MEDITERRANEAN HERITAGE

Frontispiece
Turner's Norham
Castle, Sunrise

DAVID SCOTT FOX

MEDITERRANEAN HERITAGE

ROUTLEDGE & KEGAN PAUL
LONDON, HENLEY AND BOSTON

First published in 1978
by Routledge & Kegan Paul Ltd
39 Store Street, London WC1E 7DD,
Broadway House, Newtown Road,
Henley-on-Thames, Oxon RG9 1EN and
9 Park Street,
Boston, Mass. 02108, USA
Set in 12pt on 14pt Perpetua
and printed in Great Britain by
Ebenezer Baylis and Son Ltd
The Trinity Press, Worcester, and London
© Sir David Scott Fox 1978

British Library Cataloguing in Publication Data

Fox, David Scott
Mediterranean heritage
1. Great Britain – Civilization – Classical
influences   2. Great Britain – Civilization –
Italian influences
I. Title
941   DA110   78–40392

ISBN 0 7100 8840 x

To
ITALY and GREECE

CONTENTS

PREFACE xi

INTRODUCTION 1

1 MEDITERRANEAN APPROACHES 5

2 THE RENAISSANCE 21

3 THE AGE OF THE GRAND TOUR 45

4 ARCHITECTURE 61

5 PAINTING 87

6 ART INTO LANDSCAPE 109

7 ROMANTIC YEARNINGS 121

8 VICTORIANA 139

9 IN THE PRESENT DECLENSION 151

BIBLIOGRAPHY 169

NAME INDEX 171

GENERAL INDEX 177

ILLUSTRATIONS

FRONTISPIECE

Turner's *Norham Castle, Sunrise* (Tate Gallery, London)

BETWEEN PAGES 36 AND 37

1 Page from the Canterbury Psalter, in the British Museum, showing hybrid of Celtic and classical (Mansell Collection)
2 Lindisfarne Gospels: St Mark (British Museum)
3 Westminster Abbey: tomb of Henry VII and Elizabeth of York Royal Commission on Historical Monuments (England)
4 It is not easy to believe that Shakespeare's *Rape of Lucrece* can have been entirely uninfluenced by this fresco of Giulio Romano at Mantua (Mansell Collection)
5 Sir Philip Sidney, the complete Italianate courtier (National Portrait Gallery, London)
6 Vesuvius erupting (British Museum)
7 Gillray's caricature shows Sir William Hamilton, who appears as Claudius in the painting on the wall (*right*), with Emma Hamilton as Cleopatra and Nelson as Mark Antony (Mansell Collection)
8 Tourist at Naples with natives absconding with his baggage (Mansell Collection)

ix

9 Tourists inspect Roman remains (Mansell Collection)
10 Palladio's Villa Rotonda, Vicenza (Mansell Collection)
11 Burlington's Chiswick House, London (Mansell Collection)
12 The Whitehall Banqueting House, London (Mansell Collection)
13 Baroque grandiosity at Castle Howard (Mansell Collection)

BETWEEN PAGES 84 AND 85

14 The Etruscan Room at Osterley Park, Middlesex (National Monuments Record)
15 The disturbing naturalism of the Elgin Marbles (British Museum)
16 The British Museum, with its forest of Greek columns (Mansell Collection)
17 The Reform Club, an example of Charles Barry's taste for the Roman (Mansell Collection)
18 Pompeo Batoni's group of English tourists in Rome, about 1750 (Mellon Collection)
19 Reynolds's *Commodore Keppel* (National Maritime Museum, London)
20 Poussin's *Landscape in the Roman Campagna* (National Gallery, London)

BETWEEN PAGES 132 AND 133

21 Claude's *Aeneas at Delos* (National Gallery, London)
22 Claude's *Embarkation of the Queen of Sheba* (National Gallery, London)
23 Turner's *Dido Building Carthage* (National Gallery, London)
24 Turner's *The Bay of Baiae, with Apollo and the Sibyl* (Tate Gallery, London)
25 Turner's *Rain, Steam and Speed* (National Gallery, London)
26 Two painters' impressions of Englishmen's eighteenth-century landscapes
Turner's *Petworth Park* (Tate Gallery, London)
27 Constable's *Wivenhoe Park, Essex* (Widener Collection, National Gallery of Art, Washington)
28 Victorian tourists at Venice (Mansell Collection)

PREFACE

The aim of this book is to draw together all the main threads of the influence of Greece and Italy on the development of English culture down to the present day. I hope that it may prove helpful to readers needing a simple summary of the whole story.

INTRODUCTION

'All our religion, almost all our law, almost all our arts, almost all that sets us above savages, has come to us from the shores of the Mediterranean.' This is a remarkable admission, particularly considering that it emanated from a writer so robustly insular as Dr Johnson but, in the cosmopolitan eighteenth century when he was writing, hardly any educated Englishman would have dreamt of disputing this dictum. There still remains a good deal of truth in it today, even if it may now seem far less self-evident.

In many ways, though not of course in all, our modern world is a continuation of the old world of Greece and Rome. Its scientific achievements are its own. But the spiritual achievements of our civilization would have been inconceivable without those of ancient Greece and Rome and their revival at the time of the Italian Renaissance. England's religion was not only born in a Mediterranean country but acquired its organized framework from Greek and Roman philosophy, and the Anglican Church is an offshoot of the Church of Rome. The distinctive legal system developed here ultimately derives, like those of other western countries, from the tremendous monument of Roman law. In their political ideals, too, the English remain the heirs of Greece and Rome, even though the Greeks, who invented democracy and from whom we took the term, did not ascribe to this particular form of government all the sovereign virtues that we do ourselves.

The English vocabulary possesses its inimitable richness because it has borrowed so extensively from other languages, particularly the classical. This has made it an admirable instrument for the poet, giving him as it were a double keyboard on which to play. Shakespeare was one of those who knew how to make use of this to enrich his verse with a counterpoint of Anglo-Saxon and Latin words; not only do they possess a contrasting music, but the former seem to speak first and foremost to our hearts and the latter more directly to our minds.

It would not be difficult to prolong this catalogue. But this book is primarily concerned with only one aspect of England's many-sided debt to Italy and Greece. Its main theme will be to trace the effects of the fertilizing influences which have repeatedly reached her art and literature from these Mediterranean countries ever since the beginnings of her history. As can still be perceived from the loveliest vestiges of our past, many of the glories of British civilization took their inspiration from Italian or Greek models. There is nothing discreditable in making such an admission. For if English art was often derivative, it has, on the other hand, very seldom been merely imitative. The English learnt to assimilate the influences which came to them from abroad, evolving national idioms of their own which frequently ended by surpassing the foreign originals from which they sprang.

But art and literature cannot be viewed in isolation. Art forms express an attitude to life, and Mediterranean influences not only persisted in the arts and in letters but had an age-long impact on the English mind itself. Although the racial ancestry of the English was Nordic, their cultural ancestry is predominantly Mediterranean. As Anglo-Saxons they are essentially a practical people, more given to pragmatism than to theory. The talents of their poets and artists have often been too introspective and personal to absorb very happily the idealistic naturalism of the Mediterranean tradition. Occasional failures in communication were inevitable. None the less, there can be no doubt that the disciplines of Mediterranean classicism were what the English most needed in order to counterbalance their instinctive romanticism, whilst Latin rationalism could best provide the complement to the imaginative qualities which they inherited from the Celts. It is in the synthesis of all these contrasting trends that the secret of the particular genius of the English people is to be found.

Italy must of necessity figure more prominently than Greece in the story that follows. In the great age of Greece, Britain was still only a remote and barbarous island. Later the situation was virtually reversed; for by the time our own civilization had evolved, Greece had in turn become one of the least enlightened and accessible countries in Europe. After the Renaissance, which passed Greece by, British contacts with Italy became far closer, particularly in the arts, whilst ancient Greece continued to remain for us only a remote, nostalgic dream.

But the Greeks had been concerned with the all-important question, 'what is the best way of life for man?' The radiance of the Greek spirit was never completely obscured in the eyes of the rest of Europe. It illuminated our spiritual Odyssey and seemed for generations to represent sweetness and light, in contrast to the growing materialism of the modern world. Thus, the English life of the mind owed an imperishable debt to Greek as well as to Italian influences. Their strands were often interwoven. Together they make up the pattern of this country's Mediterranean heritage linking its civilization to the common patrimony of Europe, which forms the theme of this book.

If it is true that an understanding of the past can assist us to come to terms with the present, then this subject may not be without a certain topicality at a time when the British are beginning to realize that their future is bound up with Europe. I have always liked to believe that there ought not to be anything particularly daunting about the idea that we shall have to become 'good Europeans'. After all, this would be nothing so very new. For centuries, the British were proud to consider themselves part of Europe, whose ancient civilizations helped to mould their own. In countless different ways they belonged to Europe in the past. So long as they remember this heritage, they may feel less cause for alarm at the prospect of taking their place in the Europe of tomorrow.

CHAPTER I

MEDITERRANEAN APPROACHES

One aspect of history is the progressive expansion of the human horizon. In the beginning, every man must have been what John Donne called 'an island, entire of itself', a lonely isolated figure in a hostile world. He can have had no knowledge of anything beyond the limits of his little group, his tribe. Increasingly, over many thousands of years, the individual has been able to enlarge his awareness, and ultimately his human faculties and creative powers. In the end, man's world has become commensurate with the universe itself, so that today men are able to feel themselves involved in the fate of peoples in far distant countries and watched with breathless excitement when the astronauts revealed the secrets of outer space.

This has, however, been the culmination of an exceedingly gradual and arduous process of development. In this remote island on the marches of Europe, it proceeded at first far more slowly than for the peoples of the Mediterranean, who had created complex societies at a period when the British themselves were still a very primitive people. It was from these civilizations that our own was at last to come. But before considering what British culture has in more recent times owed to Greece and Italy, it will help put the picture in perspective to sketch the bare outlines of its earlier connections with them.

It may still be uncertain whether or not the original inhabitants of Britain formed part of a Mediterranean race, which brought with them the rudiments of civilization, including a knowledge of agriculture, weaving and pottery. In any event, the island's earliest contacts with the Mediterranean world go back to near the beginnings of its history. Already Stonehenge appears to contain traces of what may be Mediterranean refinements, including a carved dagger of Mycenaean pattern. Herodotus refers to Britain, which he calls the 'Tin Islands', and it was the repute of the Cornish tin mines that first attracted Mediterranean traders to British shores. From at least as early as the fifth century BC, moreover, at the time when Herodotus was writing, successive waves of Celtic infiltrations were bringing the British into contact with a culture which stretched across Europe as far as the Aegean. With the La Tène Celts there came not only the iron swords which made them invincible against the Bronze Age islanders, but also art of extraordinary sophistication by the standards of that remote period. We now find the native art of Britain containing motifs derived from Italy and even decorations, like the honeysuckle ornament, which can ultimately be traced back to classical Greece itself. During the centuries which followed, the Nordic strain in British art often remained predominant, and was indeed responsible for many of its highest achievements; but more southerly influences were rarely entirely absent.

Until the Roman invasion such civilizing influences touched Britain comparatively lightly however. Then came a dramatic change: suddenly the Roman occupation in the first century of the Christian era merged the island into the greatest Mediterranean empire which the world has ever known. The existing British society of warring tribes was transformed by Roman laws and customs, institutions and organization. The British were able to share in the benefits of the most highly developed civilization in Europe. Compared with what had preceded and what was to follow, this seems a golden age in this country's history.

The Romans brought not only law and order, but new religions and at least a veneer of learning and culture as well. The refined and literate Latin language became adopted by the Romanized Celtic upper class, even though the majority of the population no doubt contented themselves with a far less sophisticated form of speech. British art received a new direction too, classical naturalism and realism gradually replacing the more poetic curvilinear abstractions of the Celtic style.

Rome was also responsible for the country's first proper architecture. In pre-Roman times, towns had been unknown here. Now, cities and luxurious villas similar to those in Italy sprang up in the English countryside, and the capital city of London itself was founded by the Romans. Each city was modelled on the Roman pattern, containing a forum or town centre, a basilica, and amenities like public baths, theatres, schools, inns and restaurants. The houses were substantial and elaborate constructions, with decorated walls and mosaic floors whose designs were derived from Italy, and ultimately from Greece and the Hellenistic world from which Roman culture had borrowed so lavishly.

Although the Roman civilization was essentially urban, it is not only their first towns that the British owed to the Romans, but also their first country houses. Agriculture had already been flourishing before the Roman occupation, and many Britons continued with their traditional way of life, whilst taking advantage of the wide variety of new fruits and domestic animals introduced by the Romans. However, recent excavations, such as those at Fishbourne and Lullingstone, have shown that the Roman-style villas now built by the richer farmers were on an ambitious scale, with much the same amenities and decorations as the town houses. It is evident that the Mediterranean style of gracious living was eagerly adopted by such Britons as could afford it.

For nearly four centuries, almost one-fifth of our whole recorded history, Britain remained a Roman province. It would be too little merely to say that she was influenced by the Mediterranean world throughout that long period: for all practical purposes, she was absorbed in it. Britain formed an integral part of a great empire based on Rome, where travel and trade were free. To call himself a citizen

of Rome was the proudest title to which a Briton could aspire, and he
would have been able to feel at home anywhere in Roman Europe.

As so often, however, civilization proved a very fragile thing, and
it seems likely that the civilization imposed by our conquerors had
touched mainly the élite and never penetrated very deeply. Already
in the fourth century the Imperial administration started to disintegrate under the pressure of barbarian raids. The Roman interlude
in Britain's history finally came to an end when the legions were
withdrawn in AD 410 and the Emperor Honorius told the British
'civitates' that they must see to their own defence. The achievements
of centuries of Roman occupation were obliterated with frightening
rapidity. The towns lay abandoned; the villas in ruins; and soon few
vestiges of Rome remained, apart from her imperishable roads.
Desolation and anarchy reigned in place of civilization and order.
The Mediterranean light had been extinguished, although an after-glow
may perhaps have been palely reflected in the Arthurian legends. The
Dark Ages had begun.

None the less, not quite everything was lost. Fortunately for
European civilization, the Church of Rome survived the fall of the
Empire, becoming in many respects its successor; and its spiritual
dominion over the minds and hearts of men was more profound and
broadly based than that of the Caesars. Nearly a hundred years before
the end of the Roman occupation, Christianity had been recognized
by Constantine and had soon afterwards become the official Imperial
religion, so that this faith, born and developed on the shores of the
Mediterranean, had had time to take root in Britain. It was never
totally destroyed here even in the chaos which followed the departure
of the legions.

The Papacy was not indifferent to the survival of British Christianity
in its hour of need, and Pope Gregory the Great sent St Augustine
and Paulinus to spread the gospel. Superficial though their immediate
success proved to be, the Christian faith slowly extended its hold in
Britain. In the year 664, the Synod of Whitby finally decided against
the rival Irish faction and in favour of Rome, thus wholeheartedly
embracing the wider world of the Mediterranean; and by the end of

the seventh century, when Hadrian and Theodore, two other emissaries from Italy, had completed the first organization of the English Church, many of the pagan Anglo-Saxons had been converted and Christianity had become firmly established.

Thus England came to form part of a Christian world which still breathed something of the spirit of the vanished Empire. Her membership of the universal and indivisible Church, with its international institutions and language, created a permanent connection between this island and the rest of Europe, so that England would never find herself entirely isolated in the future. Once again she was merged in an international organization based on Rome, and with a link with Italy which ensured that the continuity between her civilization and the ancient world should never be wholly severed.

In a sense, this might be described as the second, and more lasting, Mediterranean conquest of Britain. From that time until the end of the Middle Ages, a major role in English history was played by the Church of Rome and by the Latin civilization which it represented. The greatest power on the whole continent of Europe, the Church was often more than a match for the State, and the King himself would hesitate to challenge the authority of the Pope, who was his Father in God. The Church, moreover, provided a refuge for what little remained of culture and scholarship after the collapse of Roman civilization, and it can even be claimed that it was on England and Ireland that the first span of the bridge was built which would ultimately connect the medieval culture of Europe with the classical.

In order to spread the faith it was essential to spread the language of the gospel. So the Church found itself obliged to enter the educational field in a systematic fashion. Scholars were sent from Rome to set up schools where the newly converted Anglo-Saxon clergy were taught not only the Latin script and language, which became the basis of Anglo-Saxon education, but also the rudiments of classical as well as Christian literature. Thanks to this diffusion of Latin through the Church and the monasteries, some international learning and culture was able to survive even in the darkest times, and when early English literature began to develop, it was largely founded on Latin precedents.

The Church thus brought Mediterranean learning and ideas to the unlettered barbarians. It was also soon to be the main vehicle for reviving Roman influences in the arts. Even the rough Anglo-Saxon invaders could hardly fail to be impressed by the magnificent Roman buildings which they found in Britain; derelict though these were, enough was left to influence and inspire. From as early as the seventh century, when the Church and its Benedictine missionaries began to take the cultural lead, there are examples of primitive Anglo-Saxon churches modelled on Roman lines, built in stone instead of wood and sometimes with their ground-plan conforming to Italian prototypes. Masons from Rome worked on the great ecclesiastical buildings in Northumbria, and the first of the English churches in the basilican manner were built at Hexham, Ripon and York.

The barbarian invaders of the Empire had brought with them new art forms of their own, however; and after Rome's final collapse, it had seemed for a time that Roman artistic influence in western Europe might also succumb. The art of England herself was dominated by the so-called 'Celtic' style, which had been developed in the monasteries of Ireland. With its emphasis on line rather than form, and on mysticism instead of realism, this was in many ways the antithesis of the Roman tradition, and is believed to have owed more to Germany and Coptic Egypt, or even to Syria, than it did to Rome. Its intricate interlaced designs and brilliantly abstract patterns (which sometimes include fabulous beasts, reminiscent of German or Scandinavian art) were often of great technical skill, with a lyrical power and a peculiar beauty of their own.

But it was not very long before Rome's artistic influence began to revive in England as elsewhere in the West. There was a gradual return to the older and more humanistic Mediterranean styles. The latter had no monopoly, however, for Celtic and other influences did not altogether relinquish their hold. So there were often curious compromises, as when the borders of a painting are in the Celtic manner, but an almost classical figure forms its centrepiece. It was to be several centuries before the synthesis of these very different styles, which is known as the 'Romanesque', was finally achieved.

Meanwhile, already in the early Middle Ages, English monks and pilgrims had begun to visit Italy and to bring back not only manuscripts, which were industriously copied in the English monasteries, but sometimes also pictures and works of art to adorn the English churches. The clergy needed representations of Christ and the saints to illustrate the Bible story; and a revolutionary change occurred after the Synod of Whitby when the Roman Church introduced the human figure, the essential Mediterranean art form, into Anglo-Saxon sacred art.

It has been suggested, too, that Roman sculptural remains may have inspired the sculptors who worked in seventh- and eighth-century England at a time when sculpture in the round was hardly being produced anywhere else in Europe; and the great stone crosses like that at Ruthwell, which are amongst the finest relics of Anglo-Saxon Christianity, were sometimes decorated with motifs evidently derived from Rome and Byzantium. The influence of Mediterranean naturalism can also be seen in the illuminated manuscripts which were in time to acquire a European reputation; and the famous Lindisfarne Gospels themselves show Italian inspiration. Although the style of painting developed in the monasteries shows the strong Celtic influence and might even be characterized as in many ways typically English, its sources were generally continental manuscripts which carried on the Mediterranean traditions.

With the Roman faith, therefore, ultimately came Roman-derived art. Much in the history of English art between AD 800 and 1200 might be summarized by saying that our artists (like those in the rest of western Europe) were working out how to reconcile their native ways of creating things with the methods and ideals of Mediterranean and Byzantine art. Frequently, classical forms would be used in a very unclassical manner, in order to express Nordic ideas far removed from those of Rome. But whereas in architecture, sculpture and painting, Roman influences were assimilated to local styles, in music, on the other hand, the Roman inspiration was practically exclusive. The Romanization of Anglo-Celtic music is described in some detail by the Venerable Bede, the eighth-century Northumbrian monk and scholar. The Roman chant, codified by Gregory the Great, stands at the beginning of the history of English music, and for a long time church music provided the only organized form of musical culture. This was music in the Roman manner, the new music introduced from Rome in the seventh century.

Thus, under the protection of the Church, some legacies of ancient Rome survived. Within the framework provided by ecclesiastical institutions, civilization could gradually revive. Finally, there came a period during the Dark Ages when the light of learning burnt more brightly in our island than anywhere on the continent of Europe. By the eighth century a new tradition of scholarship had grown up around the Benedictine monasteries which owed so much to Rome. Although the Latin language and the scriptures naturally held pride of place, increasing attention was paid to pagan as well as Christian literature. English churchmen like Aldhelm, Boniface and Bede became famous throughout Europe for their learning and their missionary zeal. Their missionary activities had lasting consequences for northern Europe, particularly those of St Wilfrid, who proselytized the heathen Frisians in 678–9, and of Boniface, who worked on the continent for twenty years in the middle of the eighth century under the direction of Rome, helping King Pepin the Short to reorganize the West German and Frankish Churches.

Scholars such as these were now to bring the erudition derived from their study of classical literature to the court of the great Frankish empire at the very heart of western Christendom. So high was their prestige that it was to England that Charlemagne looked for a model when he undertook the radical reformation of the educational system in his own dominions in order to revive classical learning in continental Europe. He persuaded Alcuin, the master of the great cathedral school at York, then the centre of English scholarship, to become head of the palace academy at his Frankish court at Aachen and undertake the direction of his reforms, with the result that the pattern established at York had been adopted in the new schools of Carolingian Europe by the end of the eighth century.

The Carolingian period saw a further cross-fertilization between

English and Mediterranean culture. The native love of decoration had once again been gaining ground at the expense of classical realism, but Carolingian influences brought a return to greater naturalism, so that British art now became a branch of the European art which was based on the classical heritage. Although the development of this Mediterranean-oriented civilization was soon to be brutally interrupted by the beginning of the Viking raids, a revival took place in the time of Alfred the Great. He re-established English ties with Rome, which he had twice visited as a boy, and his love of art and literature led him to invite Italian craftsmen to England and to commission a number of new translations of Latin manuscripts, including the philosophical works of Boethius, in the hope that they would contribute to the instruction and edification of his people.

Any respite from the Vikings was usually short-lived, however, and the preconditions for a genuine renaissance were lacking in that troubled age. None the less, learning was never completely extinguished; and during the tenth century, when there was again a rather more tranquil and prosperous period for England, St Dunstan's monastic reforms, bringing stricter observance of the Benedictine rule and renewed emphasis on education and the arts, stimulated fresh contacts with the Mediterranean world.

But it was not until after the Norman conquest that England at last became safe from the Viking pressure which had threatened to separate her from the Roman world and submerge her in a Scandinavian empire. Although the Normans themselves originated in Scandinavia, they had long been converted to Latin culture. The year 1066 was a watershed in the history of our island, for William the Conqueror then finally put it beyond doubt that England's destiny would lie with western and not northern Europe and that she would remain one of the heirs of Rome.

In Norman times, Christianity and the spiritual authority of Rome welded Europe together even more strongly than in the days of Charlemagne. The Norman nobility belonged to the Romanesque world which believed that God's Kingdom must be set up here upon earth. They were also political realists who understood the importance of enlisting the support of the Church of Rome. It was as standard bearers of the Papacy that they conquered in Calabria and Sicily, and when he invaded England in 1066 William I took care to secure the Pope's blessing on his enterprise, almost as if it had been a crusade.

This was the age of the great reforming movement of Pope Gregory VII, which increased the power of the Papacy and the effectiveness of the monastic system, strengthening the hold of the Church on people's lives. William himself was a zealous ecclesiastical reformer. With the assistance of Lanfranc and Anselm, two outstandingly able Italians who successively became Archbishop of Canterbury, the antiquated Saxon Church was reorganized in accordance with the continental pattern, so as to form one of the pillars of the new government. Thus the English Church was brought much closer to the wider life of Christendom, becoming an integral part of the Church in Europe, with its great heritage of Latin culture and learning.

Politically as well, the Norman conquest bound England once again to the continent of Europe. By the middle of the twelfth century, Angevin England could almost have been described as a Mediterranean power: Henry II's dominions stretched as far as Toulouse; a flourishing wool trade was conducted with Italy; and the Crusades were involving the English in Mediterranean affairs. There was a constant flow of travellers between England and the South, monks and pilgrims, courtiers and crusaders, and increasingly merchants and scholars as well: one notable example is the great twelfth-century humanist, John of Salisbury, who would boast that he had 'ten times passed the chain of the Alps'. Many Scots also found their way to Italy, although the story of King Macbeth's pilgrimage to Rome is probably only apocryphal.

Contacts between Canterbury and Sicily were particularly close. Just as Italians had been appointed to high ecclesiastical offices in England, so English churchmen, like Walter of the Mill, the all-powerful Archbishop of Palermo, and other Englishmen were prominent in the Sicilian administration. The marriage of the Norman King of Sicily to an English princess, the daughter of Henry II, set the seal on the relationship between the two courts, and a century later Henry III even attempted to acquire the Sicilian crown for his own family. It was through Sicily, too, that England received much of the Byzantine influence frequently to be found in the splendid illuminated manuscripts of the period, such as the Winchester Bible.

All things considered, it must have redounded to England's advantage to find herself orientated towards western and southern Europe rather than in the narrower orbit of Scandinavia, even though the long wars with France were a heavy price to pay. Culturally as well, the Norman conquest brought more gain than loss on balance. No doubt it meant the end of much that was precious in the old England, and it was not until Chaucer that English literature could once more fully equal what had been achieved, on the basis of Christian and classical culture, by the Anglo-Saxon poets in the days before the Danish and Norman invasions. By Norman times, however, anarchy was threatening the survival of what was left of the ancient English culture. The harshly authoritarian government of William I did at least serve to give England an essential measure of stability.

At the same time, the conquest opened the way for England to participate in a broader European civilization. Although her main link with the continent was France and not Italy, her new rulers were themselves a Latinized people whose language was Latin-derived. Latin itself survived as the language of the Church and of scholars, and would long so remain. Still a living speech, it was the international language not only of clerics and philosophers, but also of scientists and diplomatists and of polite conversation. To write meant to write in Latin, the international medium of all intellectual life; and even today it is sometimes said that 'the English speak Anglo-Saxon but write Latin'. Thus we never completely lost touch with our classical heritage; and Latin as well as French came to play an important part in moulding the development of our English language.

The civilization of the Normans owed a great deal to the Mediterranean world in which their Italian possessions gave them a stake. Through their intermediary there flowed to England new cultural influences from Italy and farther east. This country now felt the full

impact of the continental Romanesque style, especially in the tremendous outburst of building which followed the Norman conquest.
The invaders gave to English architecture a disciplined nobility such
as had been beyond the reach of the essentially provincial Saxon
manner. Their cathedrals at Durham and elsewhere were of ponderous
and imposing splendour, unsurpassed even by the great churches built
at this period at Bari and Pisa in Italy itself.

By the eleventh century, Romanesque art, born long before in the
Benedictine monasteries of northern Italy, had emerged as a coherent
international style. As its name implies, it looked to Roman models,
although it also derived a great deal from both the eastern Mediterranean and the 'barbarian' North. The Romanesque architects built
with a Roman solidity. They developed the groin-vaulting which had
already been in use in Roman times. It was, however, the column,
virtually the only ornament of this austere style, which was the main
legacy inherited from classical architecture; and after the massive
Norman variety, and before the final Gothic refinement, there was a
brief interval when the shafts had proportions of more authentic
classical elegance, sometimes with Corinthian capitals, such as may be
seen, for instance, in the choir of Canterbury cathedral.

But the Normans' version of this Romanesque style did not only
emulate the Roman ideals of serenity and permanence. Their art also
reflected the Byzantine aspiration to create a symbolic semblance of
eternity. The sculptures at Malmesbury and Chichester, like the
suggestions of Arab craftsmanship occasionally found in other English
churches of this period, show that they were the work of a people
who had relatively close links with the countries of the eastern
Mediterranean. Contacts had been established by English traders and
pilgrims, but it was first and foremost the Crusades that revealed to
western Europe the wonders of Byzantine and Moslem civilization.

Meanwhile in architecture, however, the static Romanesque and
Byzantine conventions were to be discarded, once the revolutionary
invention of the pointed arch made possible the construction of soaring
buildings of a gracefulness more in harmony with the changing spirit
of the age. Although there may have been some Arab influence in its

origins, the new Gothic style, which gave England so many of her finest churches, marks something of a break with Mediterranean traditions. For it came to us not from Italy but from France where it had emerged at St-Denis in about 1135. It belonged essentially to northern Europe, and Italian Gothic developed outside the main stream. But medieval craftsmen could hardly help weaving something of the Greco-Roman past into the new framework. An almost classical idealization can be found in certain early Gothic sculpture, evidently inspired by antique Roman models. Even a hint of Arab influence still seems apparent in the Perpendicular style which was to represent the principal English variation on the Gothic theme.

Throughout the Middle Ages, when intellectual life was centred on the monasteries, the Church of Rome remained the principal patron not only of architecture and the arts, but also of learning. With the help of the Church and of what had survived from Rome, the rough islanders could gradually learn the rudiments of civilization. In England, as elsewhere in the West, the Mediterranean legacy was continuously shaping institutions, thought and culture. Although antiquity was alien to this Christian age in so far as it was pagan, even the Church itself was unable to escape its fascination, seldom failing to encourage the careful pursuit of classical knowledge. Medieval man found himself living in a world manifestly inferior to the ancient, whether in political organization or mastery of the material environment. For those who cared about such things, there seemed little doubt that the destruction of the Roman Empire had meant the end of civilized life itself. Even if the golden age of Rome was now gone beyond recall, some at least of its secrets might be revealed by searching amongst the precious relics of the classical past. The medieval ambition was less to invent a new world than to rebuild in imitation of the old, by rediscovering its forgotten wisdom.

The astonishing renaissance during the twelfth century, when the nightmare of the Dark Ages was at last coming to an end, once again brought Mediterranean influences to the fore. This was a time of intellectual ferment, and the thirst for knowledge led to a great awakening of Latin learning. Europe's first universities were now being founded, so that scholarship was no longer confined to the monasteries and choir schools. After Salerno and Bologna had shown the way, the Italian example was followed at Oxford and subsequently at Cambridge. There were Italians, like Vacarius the Lombard jurist, amongst the famous scholars who came from the continent to teach; and following the arrival at Oxford of Franciscan friars from Italy in the thirteenth century, there was a remarkable development of intellectual life which would produce a line of outstanding English philosophers.

Central to the curriculum here as in the rest of western Europe, was the study of the Latin authors and of such few Greek works as had survived in the West. For in the eyes of all those seeking to recover the literature, art, craftsmanship, science and administration which had been lost after the civilization of Rome had succumbed to the barbarians, the classics were the accepted fountainhead of wisdom. Already in the Dark Ages, when England was for a time the most advanced country in Europe, men had yearned for the classical past. The seventh-century Latin poems of Aldhelm, England's first scholar of international distinction, were, for example, often a reflection of those of Virgil; Bede's great history had described the collapse of civilization after the fall of the Roman Empire, and its subsequent recovery from barbarism; whilst King Alfred's Latin translations have already been mentioned.

Even when life gradually became more urbane, scholarship still concentrated on the Greek and Latin authors, and particularly the writings of Aristotle, however strangely they might often be interpreted. Though the backward-looking medieval philosophy was eventually overtaken by the paralysis of scholasticism, their classical studies did at least serve to train men's minds to think with greater logical precision, so that the seeds of modern science had been sown.

The classical dream, haunting the European imagination through the centuries, and the immense importance which all educated men attached to the ancient wisdom, was only one element in the cultural homogeneity of the Middle Ages. Our own island, on the northern periphery of Latin Christendom, shared in a civilization which owed its remarkable coherence above all to the fact that it was firmly based on Christianity. The universal Church of Rome, with its army of ecclesiastics bound together through their orders, their virtual monopoly of scholarship and their Latin speech, provided the medieval world with its essential unity. It imposed a common standard of culture and learning deriving largely from the classical past.

But the extraordinary achievements of the Church during the Middle Ages sprang from pretensions so far-reaching as to be ultimately self-defeating. It was inevitable that the papal claim to absolute authority over man in this world should prove a continuing source of conflict between Church and State, the Pope in Rome and the secular monarchs. The long struggle for power between the kings and the barons gave the Papacy ample opportunities to intervene in English affairs, and it did not scruple to use them. In the hands of the Pope lay the dreaded weapons of excommunication and interdict. Thomas à Becket showed how in that age of faith a churchman could, with Rome's support, defy the most strong-willed king; whilst one of our less reputable monarchs had even gone to the length of offering to cede his sovereignty to the Pope.

The unity of Christendom had been undermined by the decline of the Papacy. It was at last to be destroyed by the growth of nationalism and of the power of the English and other Western European monarchies. In the 1530s, Henry VIII's revolt against papal domination finally led to the severance of the link with the Catholic Church which had done so much to involve England in the Roman world. But by the time this long chapter in the history of the Anglo-Italian relationship drew to its close, another was already opening. England was now on the threshold of a new age which would bring her even closer to the Mediterranean legacy than religion had done in the past. For by the beginning of the sixteenth century Italy had become identified with the highest achievements of the Renaissance, and throughout the whole of western Europe the ruling, intellectual and artistic classes were instinctively turning to her for wisdom, grace and culture.

CHAPTER 2

THE RENAISSANCE

Medieval England had essentially belonged to the Gothic North, even though, as we have already seen, she had never lived entirely isolated from Mediterranean Europe. Apart from the religious link with Rome, her principal contacts lay with her neighbours in Normandy and France, Flanders and Germany. This state of affairs did not greatly change until the sixteenth century, after Italy's renaissance of antiquity had given that country the cultural leadership of Europe. By Elizabethan times, however, Italian influences had become predominant. Many of the most glittering achievements of this resplendent age in our history are a reflection of those of Italy herself. Her example was instrumental in helping England to catch up at last in the European race for a more modern civilization, so that she gradually emerged from the lingering shadows of her medieval past into the bright Mediterranean sunshine of the Renaissance.

The new movement had been born almost two centuries before in the Northern Italian cities where growing prosperity produced a more secular and materialistic middle-class society with ideals and aspirations far in advance of the feudalism still generally prevailing elsewhere in Europe. The humanism which evolved in Italy offered liberation from the oppressive dogmatisms of the Middle Ages, restoring to man a central place in the universe, and giving him a sense of mastery over his own destiny. A quickening of the human spirit stimulated the search for wider horizons and new frontiers for mankind. The Renaissance appetite for fame, that ultimate reward of the outstanding personality, was now the spur to high endeavour.

This was the dawn of an age when startling new discoveries would help to bring a radical transformation in western life and thought. The Renaissance spirit of sceptical enquiry prepared the way for the future scientific revolution, as well as playing a part in the religious revolution of the Reformation. In practically every field Italian enterprise and audacity were to the fore, even at first in the geographical discoveries which were eventually to change so much more than geography. The Americas were discovered by an Italian, and from another, Amerigo Vespucci, they took their name, whilst it was a Genoese, Giovanni Caboto, who in Henry VII's reign led the earliest English expedition to cross the Atlantic. Such men helped to give the world a new dimension which would soon shift the balance of economic and political power away from the Mediterranean towards more westerly countries like England.

For the Italians of the early Renaissance, however, the rediscovery of Europe's classical heritage held a more compelling fascination than any dreams of New Worlds awaiting discovery beyond the seas. Seeing themselves as heirs of ancient Rome and Athens, they seized on the remains of antiquity to guide and inspire them, and the new learning of the Renaissance 'Rebirth' began as a resurrection of the old. In the Middle Ages the ancient world had been a magical, misty vision and Plato and Homer little more than awe-inspiring names; but now fresh manuscripts came to light, including many rescued from Constantinople before it finally succumbed to the Turks in 1453, so that the glory of Greek civilization was at last more fully revealed.

The humanist scholars turned to the classics with the same avidity as the medieval schoolmen but, being less preoccupied with niceties of law and Aristotelian metaphysics, they read them with very different eyes. The literatures of Greece and Rome were by this time revered as a unique accumulation of human wisdom which could teach not only artistic elegance and style, but also a sense of moral values. Here, it was confidently believed, men would be able to rediscover the secrets of the two most cherished aspirations of the age: a richer, more civilized way of living, and artistic excellence with all its ennobling virtues.

With the antique providing ideals of perfect form for architects, sculptors and often even painters, the Renaissance produced an extraordinary ferment of artistic activity and experiment. Poetry enjoyed a special place of honour in the Italian concept of the good life, and Petrarch had been the herald of the dawn of the new era. So too it fell to the poet Geoffrey Chaucer to be the first great Englishman to voice the spirit of Renaissance Italy. Often called 'the father of English poetry', he can indeed practically be said to have invented it in its more modern form. But besides his genius as a poet, Chaucer was a man of wide sophistication, whose accomplishments as a courtier and diplomat, together with his gift for languages, marked him out for missions abroad. The three diplomatic assignments which took him to Italy must have been particularly valuable to his artistic education, as they enabled him to see the Renaissance on the eve of its brilliant beginning.

Chaucer was the first English poet who knew Europe. Although this Londoner was English to the core, in his culture he was cosmopolitan; and his poetry shows an easy, if rather sketchy, familiarity with Italian and Latin literature (as well, of course, as with the French, which was central to medieval culture). In Italy's 'dolce stil nuovo' he found elements to stimulate his genius. Much as he admired 'Fraunceys Petrark, the laureat poete', it was 'the grete poete of Itaille that highte Dant' whom he reverenced as the supreme master, and his contemporaries even claimed that he had 'written Dante in English'. Chaucer himself, however, seems to have realized that his genius was of a lesser order. He felt closer to Boccaccio. Amongst his borrowings from the latter is the plot of his *Troilus and Criseyde*. And it is tempting to imagine, although there seems to be no direct evidence to support such a theory, that it might have been the *Decameron*, with its series of stories told to while away the time, which gave him the idea for his own *Canterbury Tales*.

Chaucer had brought us to the threshold of the Renaissance. But he remained an isolated figure and founded no school of poetry such as Dante and Petrarch had done in Italy. It was not long before the gracious and cultivated society for which he wrote became engulfed in the turmoil of the Wars of the Roses. During the following century there could be little place in England for poetry and art or for any of the gentler influences which might have reached us from Renaissance Italy. All that survived to keep the new humanism alive was a handful of dedicated scholars, mainly centred on Oxford, many of whom had received their training in Italian universities.

It was not until the beginning of the reign of Henry VIII that this country could experience a brief Renaissance springtime. At first, the humanist spirit appeared well established at his court, where men like Wolsey were lavish patrons of the new learning. Already his father, Henry VII, had commissioned the Florentine sculptor, Pietro Torrigiano, to carve his tomb at Westminster, a pure Renaissance masterpiece in the midst of Gothic England, and Henry VIII himself made use of Italian artisans to help with the construction of the royal palaces. He built with a genuine feeling for Renaissance splendour.

But in the end Henry VIII failed to fulfil his initial promise of becoming a great Renaissance prince. Whilst he revelled in ostentatious display, and although he was himself an accomplished musician, he seems to have had little genuine feeling for the fine arts generally and Italian influences were never able to take a very strong hold at the court. With religious and political conflict clouding the English Renaissance almost from the start, the group of brilliant humanists of the generation of Colet and Erasmus were soon to be scattered by the storms of the Reformation.

England had to wait until more settled times returned before she was at last able to feel the full impact of the Italian Renaissance, which during the previous century had already been spreading to other western countries across the Alps. After Elizabeth I had come to the throne in 1558, however, there was a great awakening of English interest in Italy and the astonishing new world of arts and letters, philosophy and science, which had been created there. For the Elizabethans, Renaissance Italy became synonymous with the civilized and cultured refinement which they were so eager to acquire themselves. Courtiers, diplomats, poets and musicians soon concluded that it was there that they could best find their models.

By the beginning of the seventeenth century, Italian influences were making themselves felt in most sectors of English life and providing impetus and form to England's own Elizabethan Renaissance. One of the channels through which they reached the English was the flourishing colony of Italians living in London, many of whom were refugees from religious persecution at home. In the main it was a community of businessmen, which included such distinguished and influential figures as Sir Horatio Pallavicino, banker, political agent and even architect to Queen Elizabeth. The Italians had long been the most expert traders and bankers in Europe. It was they who first taught us our business. A relic of those times is the name of Lombard Street, still borne by one of the principal banking streets in the City of London, and many of our modern commercial and financial terms betray their Italian origin: for instance, bank and bankrupt, cash (from 'cassa') and £.s.d., the abbreviations for 'liri', 'soldi' and 'denarii'.

But not all the Italians in England were men of affairs. There was another type of visitor who made a particular contribution to the dissemination of Renaissance culture. Artists and craftsmen had started to arrive from Italy ever since the days of Henry VII, and Queen Elizabeth herself often favoured Italians as secretaries or court musicians. Italian doctors and lawyers were also in great demand in Elizabethan London. Italy's cultural prestige probably gained most, however, from eminent men of letters like John Florio, who not only helped to make the Italian language fashionable in England but even directly influenced the development of our own literature.

At the same time there was a flow of English visitors to Italy who did even more than the Italians here in England to familiarize the Elizabethans with the Renaissance cultural revolution. Italy's universities enjoyed a high reputation, and a growing number of young

Englishmen crossed the Alps to study, especially at Padua, where the university of the Venetian Republic had become the centre of the new classical scholarship. It was now beginning to be the fashion for the best families to try to send their sons to Italy, for it was recognized that some knowledge of the Renaissance was practically indispensable, not only for a career at the court or in diplomacy, but also to a poet, artist or even a physician. The new vogue was encouraged by the Queen herself who subsidized the foreign travels of promising young courtiers. Another to give the weight of his approval was Francis Bacon, whose essay 'Of Travel' offered excellent advice to the young on how to make the most of their time abroad. 'Travel in the younger sort', he insisted, 'is a part of education', and although this may seem a sententious platitude to us today, the idea that 'travel broadens the mind' was new and exciting at the time.

Once back in England after a few terms at an Italian university, these young men spread the fashion for Italy and everything Italian, whether it was the Italian language, music or literature, dress or behaviour. Their foreign manners and mannerisms, aping the peacock world of Renaissance Italy, often exposed them to the ridicule of their more conservative friends at home. Sometimes they also brought back strange new ideas and morals which provoked their scandalized contemporaries to echo the Italian saying that 'the Italianate Englishman is the devil incarnate'. But puritan strictures that 'popery and foppishness' were all that was likely to be learnt from the 'Siren songes of Italie' did little to dampen the enthusiasm of young Englishmen to see for themselves this fabulous birthplace of the Renaissance. It was a unique and exhilarating experience to visit Venice or Florence where they could find a society far more sophisticated than anything they knew at home. They were dazzled by this extraordinarily gifted people who could produce such an abundance of artistic achievements and geniuses as various as Dante and Aretino, Machiavelli and Castiglione.

Italy was widely esteemed as the fountainhead of political knowledge, and it was there that the scientific modern study of politics began with the publication of Machiavelli's *Il Principe* in 1532. European thought was revolutionized by the startling new theories propounded in this first analysis of power politics, which could not fail to be of burning interest to an age when rulers were profiting from men's longing for the smack of firm government that seemed to offer the best hope for the peace and order which they so ardently desired. Here was a new phenomenon in literature. For prejudiced and emotional as Machiavelli might sometimes be, his approach to his subject was inspired by a cool objectivity which would have been inconceivable in any medieval writer.

Machiavelli fascinated the English, even though many of them may have been shocked by his cynical realism. Francis Bacon, who had rather a similar cast of mind and an equal detestation of cant, was amongst those who gave their whole-hearted approval, praising 'Machiavelli and other writers of that class who openly and unfeignedly declare and describe what men do and not what they ought to do'. Bacon's own philosophy, substituting the active ideal for the contemplative, is only one example of the profound influence which this Italian exercised on English thought. Machiavelli's name is one that constantly recurs in Elizabethan literature. In the eyes of the dramatists he symbolized the new Renaissance spirit; and his brilliant little book, containing so many provocative ideas, so lucidly developed, left an enduring impression on the English mind.

Equally influential in its very different way was Castiglione's *Il Cortegiano*, another Italian work which appeared early in the sixteenth century almost simultaneously with Machiavelli's *Prince*. The English translation enjoyed an immense vogue, and the book seems to have been considered the last word on polite behaviour even down to the time of Dr Johnson who called it 'the best book that was ever written upon good breeding'. The ideal of the perfect personality popularized by Castiglione was a Renaissance creation which was based on genuine human values. It played an important part in forming our notion of the English gentleman. Certainly, no aspiring young Elizabethan courtier could afford to neglect this expert advice on how to acquire the Italian polish and refinement which were then so highly prized.

It was in fact in England itself that there now emerged the very incarnation of the graces and accomplishments extolled by Castiglione. For Sir Philip Sidney, scholar, courtier, soldier, diplomat and poet, and richly endowed with charm and character as well, was a paragon even by the standards of his gifted generation. When he met his death through a recklessly gallant gesture at the battle of Zutphen in 1586, all Europe joined in mourning this young man who was acclaimed as 'the flower of England', 'the hope of all learned men' and 'the darling of the human race', and who had made himself so widely beloved as the quintessence of the peculiar radiance of the Elizabethan age:

> To hear him speake and sweetly smile,
> You were in Paradise the while.

Philip Sidney was given a state funeral of the utmost pomp and magnificence, his hearse 'attended by poets, and mourneful elegies and poems, with the pens that wrote them, thrown into his tomb'. Foreigners as well as Englishmen felt that they had suffered irreparable loss, not only of a great poet cut off in his prime, but of a future leader of England and of Protestant Europe. Countless elegies were written in his honour. He was long and fondly remembered, and many years after his death a fellow-poet recalled:

> *Sydnaen* showers
> Of sweet discourse, whose powers
> Can crowne old Winter's head with flowers.

The secret of the extraordinary mark which Sidney made on his contemporaries lay not only in the irresistible grace and fascination of his charismatic personality. What seems to have especially impressed them was that he represented a new type of Englishman: as one critic has expressed it, he was 'a man who had solved for himself the problem which confronted the rising generation, that of grafting Renaissance culture on to an English stock'. He could in fact be regarded as the first of the Elizabethans fully to belong to the new world of the Renaissance; and it would have been difficult to conceive a more

perfect example of the 'virtuoso' than this young Englishman, Italianate
in the best sense of the term, who combined the virtues of nobility,
Latin courtesy, scholarship and patronage of the arts.

Sidney's recognition that Italian inspiration must be essential to its
development was largely responsible for setting the Elizabethan
Renaissance on its course. He owed an incalculable debt to Italy
himself. After leaving his English universities (for he studied both at
Oxford and at Cambridge), he had obtained the Queen's permission
to finish his education with a period of foreign travel. This enabled
him to spend long enough in Italy to experience the glittering civilization which had been created there and to appreciate how much
his own country needed to learn from it. He studied for some months
at the famous university at Padua, perfecting his knowledge of
the language and eagerly absorbing Italian poetry and culture and the
classics which inspired them. He had even found time to sit to the
great Veronese in Venice: the picture has long ago vanished without
trace, but can hardly fail to have been the finest portrait painted of
any sixteenth-century Englishman.

After his three years abroad, Sidney returned home in 1575 a
cultivated European and a complete Renaissance man. Like the Italians
before them, the English were now embarking on the intoxicating
experience of discovering their own language and its power for beauty,
not least as a vehicle for poetry. Patron of poets and a very considerable
poet himself, Sidney played a leading role in fostering the new English
verse which flowered so brilliantly during the last two decades of the
century, when England became 'a nest of singing birds'.

The patriotic ambition of Sidney and of kindred spirits like Spenser
and Fulke Greville was to found a national school of poetry, following
the example already set by Italy. But these men were far from insular.
If they succeeded, almost miraculously quickly, in creating a poetic
tradition which was soon to produce geniuses of the international
stature of Shakespeare and Milton, and established English among the
great literatures of Europe, it was because their education and culture
enabled them to recognize that Italy and the classics could not only
provide noble themes but, more important still, could teach the

forms and disciplines, subtleties and refinements, which were still lacking in our own less sophisticated poetry.

Under the inspiration of Sidney and his friends, the galaxy of poets now beginning to emerge in England became strongly influenced by Italian humanism and literature. Dante always enjoyed a special reverence, but he seems to have been regarded as a rather remote and Olympian figure who by this time belonged to the past. More, it was felt, could be learnt from Petrarch; and for Spenser and other sonnet writers it was the latter who was the acknowledged master, just as he had already been for Wyatt and Surrey, the sonneteers of the generation before.

The Earl of Surrey had first pointed the way, making numerous translations and adaptations of the Italian poet. We can already detect a whisper of the Renaissance spring in his felicitous rendering of Petrarch's sonnet beginning 'Amor che nel penser mio vive e regna . . .', with his:

> Love that doth raine and live within my thought,
> And buylt his seat within my captive brest,
> Clad in the armes wherein with me he fought,
> Oft in my face he doth his banner rest.

Surrey and Wyatt were described by a contemporary as 'having travailed into Italie, and there tasted the sweete and stately measures and stile of the Italian Poesie as novices newly crept out of the schooles of Dante, Ariosto and Petrarch, greatly polished our rude and homely maner of vulgar Poesie, from that it had been before'. They had, in fact, embarked on the enterprise which Philip Sidney and his circle were to bring to fruition.

Thanks to the revival of interest in neo-Platonism, which did so much to stimulate the enthusiastic idealism of the age, the Petrarchan conception of ideal love, with earthly love reflecting its divine pattern, caught the imagination of the Elizabethans. They were therefore attracted as much by the substance as by the form of Petrarch's 'canzoni'. Many an Elizabethan poet delighted in feeling that Love had transfixed his Soul, and would address conceits to his mistress, real or ideal, in the same almost mystically ecstatic terms as Laura had once been invoked by Petrarch.

The latter was by no means the only Italian writer to influence English poetry at this crucial stage in its development. Whereas the English pastoral poets found models amongst the works of their Italian contemporaries or in the eclogues of Virgil, it was Tasso and Ariosto who were best able to provide the inspiration for a romantic epic like Spenser's *Faerie Queene*, which he had written with Sidney's encouragement and which provides one of the most striking examples of the merging of the Renaissance outlook with native cultural traditions. Spenser had a medieval feeling for the marvellous and magical. But this did not prevent him from being a humanist, and pagan in the intensity of his delight in sensual and visual beauty. Whilst reaching back to Malory and Chaucer, 'England's Arch-Poet' (as they called him) elaborated the grand design of this celebrated poem from much further afield, drawing not only on the Italian epics but also on Plato and the *Aeneid*.

Often the Elizabethans even succeeded in surpassing their models. Although they borrowed foreign themes and forms, they used them as the means for expressing the native richness of imagination and spontaneous feeling which is the hallmark of the Elizabethan Renaissance achievement. This was eminently the case with Shakespeare himself. His poetry would certainly have been a very different thing if the Renaissance had not provided him with such a wealth of Italian and classical cultural resources on which to draw. But we rightly regard him as characteristically English none the less. For his creative genius was never satisfied with mere imitation. Indeed, he assimilated so completely the literature which inspired him that it is often difficult to identify his sources. His sonnets, for instance, despite their unmistakable echoes of Petrarch and Michelangelo, remain an intensely personal document. With his plays it was the same: even though he so frequently lifted their plots wholesale from classical or Italian authors, their matchless poetry is Shakespeare's and Shakespeare's alone.

But the originality of Shakespeare's genius stands so far above dispute that it can be no disparagement to stress how inconceivable his poetic achievement would have been without the revelation of the Italian Renaissance. For example, the Renaissance fascination with antiquity is very clearly reflected in his writing. No doubt he lacked the brilliant scholarship of a man like Milton or of his friend Ben Jonson, whom Dryden described as 'deeply conversant in the ancients' and who was responsible for the often misquoted dictum that Shakespeare had 'small Latin and less Greek'. But as T. S. Eliot has pointed out, whilst he may not have been so well educated as some other writers of the period, this is less important than the fact that his education was of the same kind: it was based on the classics.

In the England of Shakespeare's day, the knowledge of Latin and Greek literature had been spread by the revival of classical studies at the universities, and although the Latin language was more generally studied than the Greek, it was, on the other hand, primarily Greece that infused the humanity of Elizabethan culture. Thus Shakespeare lived in a world where the wisdom of the ancients was respected and their poetry admired and enjoyed; they provided an ideal which men yearned to equal if not surpass. The standards and the rules were there, and he could count on the discriminating enthusiasm of his patrons and of a public, both of whom could be expected to take an equally passionate interest in poetry.

By Elizabethan times, moreover, Renaissance scholarship had produced translations of most of the classics, so that it was no problem for Shakespeare to familiarize himself with writers like Seneca, Plutarch or Ovid, even if he was unable to appreciate them fully in the original. For a dramatist who could never be bothered to invent the stories of his plays himself, such authors provided a priceless mine of inspiration. Not that Shakespeare contented himself with blindly following their texts: for instance, although the translation which Thomas North had just completed of Plutarch's *Lives of the Noble Greeks and Romans* supplied him with the basic material for his own *Antony and Cleopatra* and *Julius Caesar*, his alchemy transformed it into flights of sublime poetry which are infinitely more moving and make North's measured prose seem almost pedestrian by comparison.

For Shakespeare the classics were not merely, of course, a convenient source of ready-made plots. They meant far more to him than that. Apart from Roman history, his particular delight was in the pagan myths. He read and re-read them in the pages of his favourite Latin author Ovid (who had also, incidentally, been the favourite of Chaucer), until he knew them better than he knew his Bible; and it has been pointed out that the word 'Jove' occurs more frequently in Shakespeare's work than the word 'God' – except as an exclamation. These immortal stories, like so much else that he discovered in the treasure hoard of Greek and Roman literature, enriched his mind and fired his imagination. Classical imagery and allusions came almost as naturally to him as English. Never pedantic, he sometimes used them with less accuracy than feeling. But time and again Shakespeare made them contribute to his loveliest and most memorable effects, and they became an essential ingredient in the magic of his poetry.

Innumerable passages could be quoted to illustrate this and the other aspects of the many-sided impact of the ancient world on Shakespeare's poetic vision. Here, for instance, is the language which he chooses in order to describe the majesty of Hamlet's father:

> See, what a grace was seated on this brow;
> Hyperion's curls, the front of Jove himself,
> An eye like Mars, to threaten and command,
> A station like the herald Mercury. . . .

Or, to take another example in quite a different vein, there is this description of feminine graces from *As You Like It*:

> Helen's cheek, but not her heart;
> Cleopatra's majesty;
> Atalanta's better part;
> Sad Lucretia's modesty. . . .

Shakespeare was essentially a man of his time – a Renaissance Englishman who followed Italian humanism, not only in a devotion to the classics, but also in his preoccupation with human nature and his assertion of the dignity of man against the asceticism of medieval misanthropy. Though he lived in a society where many of the old ways of thought still lingered on, and although he was himself often fascinated by the medieval, he was first and foremost a humanist for whom the England of the Middle Ages was fast becoming ancient history. Nothing could be more natural than that one of his main themes should have been the new culture which Europe had inherited from Italy, 'great Italy' as he calls her, the country where, moreover, not so very long before the modern theatre itself had first been born in emulation of classical drama. We can be sure that he was proud to consider himself part of the enlightened Renaissance world. And although the affectations of the Italianized popinjays who were one of its most conspicuous products in Elizabethan society, might provide a favourite target for his satire, he showed no compunction in making liberal use himself of Italian words and mannerisms whenever he felt they could enrich the texture of his poetry.

The Elizabethan playwrights regarded Italy as a glamorous and dramatic country, inhabited by a highly theatrical people. It seemed to them an eminently suitable setting for the sort of blood-and-thunder melodramas in which they took such a delight, glittering nightmares that reflect the influence of the strange, gory tragedies of Seneca, the Roman Stoic. Shakespeare's own imagination was equally entranced by the South. A remarkable number of his plays are either set in Italy or inspired by Italian authors. Not only his heroes but also his heroines have an energy and passion which can only be described as Mediterranean. Even his Hamlet, 'the glass of fashion and the mould of form', is far less the Danish warrior of the story which he adapted than a Renaissance prince who believed in 'virtù' and who might have stepped out of the pages of Castiglione's *Courtier*.

Italy was clearly the country of Shakespeare's dreams, and a fascinating question is whether he ever actually found his way there himself. This hypothesis does not, of course, commend itself to the more orthodox Shakespearean critics. But there are too many gaps in our knowledge of his life for the idea to be ruled out as inherently impossible. A great deal in his work would certainly become easier to explain if we could assume that Shakespeare knew northern Italy at first hand. In *The Merchant of Venice*, for example, he depicts the Veneto with such astonishing accuracy and feeling that it is hard to believe that his knowledge of the country came only from hearsay. There are also passages in the *Rape of Lucrece* which strongly suggest that Shakespeare must have been to Mantua and seen Giulio Romano's frescoes in the Castello; whilst some of his plays like *The Taming of the Shrew* contain such graphic descriptions of actual Italian paintings that it is tempting to think that he must have seen them with his own eyes.

Obviously, however, none of this is more than purely circumstantial evidence. In spite of so many tantalizing hints that Shakespeare was writing of Italy from personal experience, there is no definite proof that this was the case or, indeed, that he ever went abroad at all. So it is admittedly more likely that his ideas of Italy were derived solely from his reading and from whatever his more travelled friends may have told him about the marvels they had discovered there. But even supposing that was in fact the sum total of the raw material out of which he conjured up his amazingly vivid pictures of the Mediterranean world, it would only go to show the extraordinary hold which the latter could exercise over the English imagination in an age steeped in the knowledge and love of Italian things.

If Shakespeare may thus far abide our question, there is no such enigma where John Milton is concerned: not only is it certain that he went to Italy but he has told us himself how much this experience meant to him. His life is far better documented and he left his own account of his leisurely Italian tour in 1638 and 1639, which would have been extended to Greece if English politics had not called him home. Less bigoted than his fellow Puritans who considered Italy 'the general receptacle of vice', he saw her on the contrary as 'the seat of civilisation and hospitable domicile of every species of erudition'. The poet in the young Milton could not fail to respond to the magic of the South, and the impressions he then stored up must have proved doubly precious later in his life, when he had gone blind and the time arrived for him to compose the glittering descriptions of natural beauty in his greatest masterpieces. One memorable example is the haunting simile in *Paradise Lost* describing the legions of fallen angels 'thick as Autumnal Leaves that strow the Brooks in *Vallombrosa*, where th'*Etrurian* shades high overarch't imbowr. . . .'

Milton's memories of the wooded hills at Vallombrosa went back to the excursion he had made to its Benedictine monastery on an autumn day very many years before, during the period when he was staying in Florence. In retrospect, his Florentine months may have seemed the most rewarding of all those he spent on his Italian travels. We know that he particularly valued the opportunities Florence provided for mixing with Italians who shared his literary interests: he was, as he afterwards recorded, 'a constant attendant at their literary parties'. Such company gave him the feeling that he belonged to the international world of letters, and when he saw how much the Tuscans had made out of a living language he was encouraged to use English instead of Latin for his own poetry.

Even afterwards, however, Milton never found it very easy to reconcile himself to the idea that ultimate and durable literary perfection could be achieved in any language other than Greek, Latin or Italian; and although writing mainly in his own tongue, he compromised by using an English which is studded with Latinisms. In his *Essay on Education* he calls Italian the only modern tongue worth studying, and he always retained his interest in Italy's literature. Significantly, two of his most important poems were given Italian titles. For his sonnets, five of which were actually written in Italian and in Petrarchan phrasing, he rejected the Shakespearean form and returned to that of Petrarch. It is hardly surprising that such a man should have felt particularly drawn to Dante, another philosopher-poet versed in the classics and the Bible. *Paradise Lost* contains many traces of his study of the *Divina Commedia*, and there are close parallels between these two great religious epics.

His Italian experiences left a deep mark on Milton; they gave him a wider, more cosmopolitan outlook and may have strengthened his resolve to achieve fame as a European poet rather than simply as a brilliant English political pamphleteer. Even more than his admiration for Italy and the Renaissance, however, it was his fervent love of the

1   Page from the Canterbury Psalter, in the British Museum, showing hybrid of Celtic and classical *(see page 10)*

2   Lindisfarne Gospels: St Mark *(see page 11)*

3 *above left* Westminster Abbey: tomb of Henry VII and Elizabeth of York *(see page 24)*

4 *below left* It is not easy to believe that Shakespeare's *Rape of Lucrece* can have been entirely uninfluenced by this fresco of Giulio Romano at Mantua *(see pages 35 and 131)*

5 *above right* Sir Philip Sidney, the complete Italianate courtier *(see pages 28ff)*

6 *below right* Vesuvius erupting *(see page 50)*

A COGNOCENTI contemplating ỹ Beauties of ỹ Antique.

7 Gillray's caricature shows Sir William Hamilton, who appears as Claudius in the painting on the wall *(right)*, with Emma Hamilton as Cleopatra and Nelson as Mark Antony *(see page 52)*

8 Tourist at Naples with natives absconding with his baggage

9 Tourists inspect Roman remains

10 Palladio's Villa
Rotonda, Vicenza (*see
page 69*)

11 Burlington's
Chiswick House,
London (see page 70

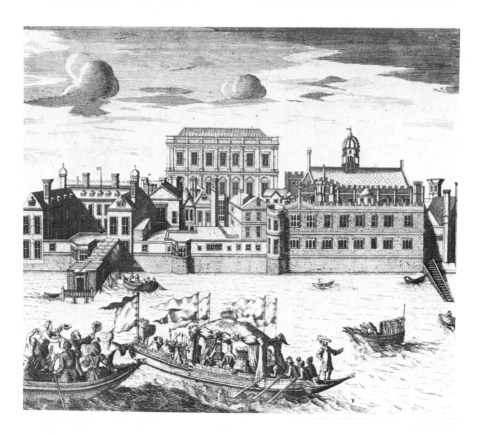

12 The Whitehall Banqueting House, London *(see page 64)*

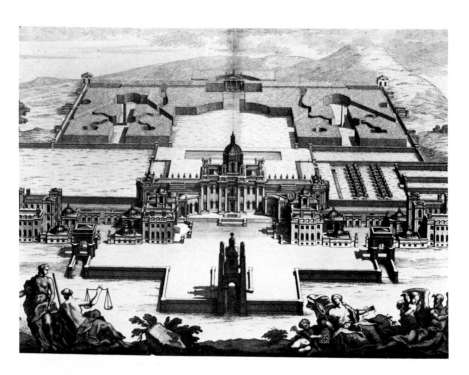

13 Baroque grandiosity at Castle Howard *(see page 67)*

classics that preserved him from the narrow obscurantism of the Puritanism of his times. All his major poems are coloured by his exceptional classical scholarship, and he is unique among the leading English poets for his continuous assimilation of the classics in his work. In *Lycidas* he followed the form of Greek pastoral poetry, whilst his *Samson Agonistes* has been described as 'a pure re-creation of Greek tragedy'.

But although Milton was always eager to acknowledge the debt which English poetry and learning owed to Greece, it is his Latinism which chiefly characterizes his writing. He could compose in Latin with great facility and imitated Horace as he has never since been imitated. His sense of language was in fact Latin rather than English. To his predilection for sonorous, polysyllabic Latin-derived words and constructions his Grand Style owes much of the splendour of its orchestration, together with any monotony and lifelessness of which it may be accused. It has even been said that without at least a rudimentary knowledge of Latin it is difficult to appreciate either the full meaning or the style and music of his poetry.

Although he was the least sacrilegious of men, Milton felt, just as Dante had done before him, that his lofty Christian purpose could be most nobly served by using classical imagery and pagan forms of expression, quoting from the classics more frequently than from the Bible itself. He delighted in taking his readers back to the ancient world, which had become so familiar to him that it seemed almost as if it were his own. Treating classical and biblical stories as virtually interchangeable, he compared Eve to one of the three goddesses on Mount Ida, and described Eden like the Garden of the Hesperides or 'that faire field of *Enna* where *Proserpin* gathring flours Her self a fairer Floure by gloomie *Dis* Was gatherd. . . .' He wrote as naturally of mythology as of the Bible, of the Greek past as of the English present, and in the noble periods of *Paradise Lost* the human implications acquire a deeper significance through this continual interplay of the sacred and the profane, the classical and the contemporary.

'Lap me in soft *Lydian* Aires, married to immortal verse', Milton sang in his *L'Allegro*. Next only to poetry, he loved music, and one of the special attractions of Italy in Milton's eyes was that it was the traditional home of music and the source of inspiration for England's own musical Renaissance. In fact there had come a time when Italy's contribution to the development of English music in some respects surpassed even that which she was making to our literature.

The defeat of the Spanish Armada in 1588 had been followed by a golden age for music as well as poetry, and for a brief interval at the beginning of the following century England could have claimed to be the leading musical nation in Europe. It was not merely that there were composers of the stature of William Byrd and Orlando Gibbons and song-writers as gifted as John Dowland. The particularly remarkable feature of this period is the way it now became a commonplace accomplishment for any gentleman or gentlewoman to sing or play some instrument, often even trying their hands at composition too. In Elizabethan England music, like poetry and dancing, was considered to have a natural place in polite education: it was something which any civilized person ought to be capable of discussing with intelligence and of composing without affectation. In all this the English were again following in Italy's footsteps. For it was there that music-making had first become part of the new Renaissance way of life, achieving the status of an almost indispensable social grace, widely cultivated in the conviction that it could enhance the moral harmony of the individual personality.

In its happiest and most spontaneous expression, Elizabethan music was combined with poetry in some of the most delightful songs ever to be written in the English language. Madrigals and ballads had been flourishing in Italy since the time of Lorenzo de' Medici; and the Italian pastoral convention had already influenced poets like Spenser. Italy's musical prestige stood extraordinarily high, so that English musicians sometimes even felt impelled to Italianize their names: the composer John Cooper, for example, visited Italy and returned determined to affect the name of 'Coperario' in future. It was quite natural, therefore, that the Elizabethan song-writers should often have chosen to take their words and music from Italian sources.

In 1588, Nicholas Younge's publication of *Musica Transalpina*, the

English translation of a collection of Italian madrigals mainly by Luca de Marenzio, heralded the splendid flowering of the English madrigal during the ensuing forty years. The Italian example was also instrumental in helping English musicians to discover new possibilities in the relationship between words and music, thus leading to the development of the 'ayre' or solo song. But if the models generally came to us from Italy, once again we ended by assimilating them and producing something as unmistakably English as Byrd's setting of 'O Mistress Mine' or Thomas Morley's 'It was a Lover and his Lass'.

In many respects, however, England still remained only on the fringes of Renaissance culture. All this dazzling outpouring of poetry and music cannot disguise the fact that the Elizabethan age, which saw the florescence of the native genius in such a variety of other fields, can scarcely be regarded as an outstandingly brilliant period for the visual arts. It is, of course, true that the English have habitually shown a greater instinctive disposition for literature than they have for painting or sculpture, and that this was by no means the only epoch in their history when the painters and sculptors were clearly outshone by the writers, and particularly by the poets, for poetry has traditionally provided the favourite vehicle for English artistic expression. In Elizabethan times, however, the contrast was sufficiently striking to demand a special explanation. It is worth pausing to consider the reasons, and why it was that both their circumstances and also their native temperament should have made it difficult for the English to respond adequately to certain aspects of the Mediterranean Renaissance.

Keenly appreciative though they were of so many of the finer things in life, the Elizabethans appear to have taken curiously little interest in either painting or sculpture from the purely aesthetic point of view. They showed a literary rather than a plastic approach to these arts which has always been characteristic of the English. Their art was irredeemably upper-class. The Renaissance cult of the individual had given portraits an enhanced importance; and like so many other upper-class Englishmen for generations to come, all that the Elizabethan patron seems to have really wanted was a flattering and dignified representation of his own person or of his family (and possibly also of his dogs and horses). Apart from the occasional allegory or miniature, painting was virtually confined to a stereotyped form of two-dimensional portraiture, which was the speciality of the Flemish artists working in England at the time. These stiff, hieratic pictures may be felt to possess a certain quaint, exotic charm of their own. Even at their best, however, they make no serious attempt to emulate the vigorous naturalism which had been Italy's great gift to the Renaissance art of Europe.

With sculpture the situation was much the same. Scarcely appreciated as an art, it was seldom in demand except for funeral effigies. Such statuary was turned out in phenomenal quantities in order to minister to the very English craving of the Elizabethans to impress posterity. With the rise of Puritanism, however, English inspiration now derived less from Catholic Italy than from the Protestant Dutch; and English sculpture remained obstinately Gothic in its conventionalized austerity and lack of feeling for the human form.

Thus this was an intensely poetic age, a musical age, but hardly a great artistic age in other respects. It was in fact to be a long time before the English visual arts could fully recover from the setback which they suffered from the Reformation, when religious images were banned and the Church lost its historic function of acting as the principal artistic patron. Now, it was the court that had become the arbiter of taste, and if it had given a proper lead, the aristocracy would no doubt have followed. But Elizabeth I, like so many other English sovereigns, was probably a philistine at heart. Although she shared the Tudor passion for pageantry and display, she does not seem to have taken much interest in art for its own sake; and in a monarchy relatively poor by Renaissance standards, any money that was to spare would be more likely to be spent on jewels or sumptuous clothes than on paintings.

Until the time of Charles I there was therefore little in England to attract the foremost foreign artists, and the only considerable Italian painter known to have paid a brief visit to this country during Elizabeth's reign is Federigo Zuccaro. Occasionally, the northern

European painters working here attempted to imitate the courtly mannerist style evolved in Florence. But nothing of great moment reached Elizabethan painting or sculpture from Italian sources, and the little that came was distorted by the Flemish channels through which it passed. All this goes far to explain the curious lack of balanced symmetry in the Elizabethan cultural achievement, for it meant that the English visual arts continued to go their own way, practically untouched by the Italian influences which were helping to raise English poetry and music to such extraordinary heights.

In sculpture, England's artistic isolation persisted for even longer than in painting; and this is not an art which can figure prominently in a brief survey of this kind designed to concentrate on those aspects of English culture which derived most benefit from Mediterranean inspiration. It is unfortunately notorious that, in recent centuries at least, the English have never been a sculptural people. They have a tendency to suffer from what Henry Moore (who is himself, of course, a brilliant exception to the general rule) has called 'form-blindness'. With their sensibilities instinctively more attuned to the appreciation of the linear tradition which they originally inherited from the Celts, it was inevitable that the Renaissance quality which came least readily to their native temperament should have been the classical sense of plastic form. Even at the best of times, it has seldom been easy for the English to achieve the Mediterranean confidence in the human body. But in the Elizabethan period, the growth of Puritanism inhibited still further their response to the Greek ideal of the nude which was such a vital ingredient in the Italian Renaissance.

There may, however, be yet another reason to help explain why the Elizabethans, who were so eager to learn from Italy in other ways, appear to have remained relatively impervious to these artistic lessons of the Renaissance. 'Poetry and Picture are arts of a like nature', wrote Ben Jonson, and Sidney called poetry a 'speaking picture', echoing the Ciceronian formula 'poema loquens pictura'. None the less, literature was in their eyes the art which deserved the higher esteem, because it could describe the 'inner mind', whereas painting, like sculpture, was limited to mere external appearances;

and in a period when poets knew how to depict scenes and people with no less vividness and colour than any Venetian painter, pictures may have seemed almost superfluous and poetry a perfectly adequate substitute. Poems of such rich descriptiveness as Shakespeare's *Venus and Adonis* and Drayton's *Endimion and Phoebe* (where the goddess spies Endimion 'neere to a Grove, where he was fishing by the River Side under a Popler, shadowed from the Sun . . .'), or the gorgeous tapestry of Spenser's *Faerie Queene*, came so close to resembling pictures that they could provide the Elizabethans with their own equivalent of Renaissance painting.

Looking back on this period, its extraordinary radiance and exuberant vitality, so brilliantly mirrored in its spate of enchanting poetry, are liable to give the superficial impression that all was sweetness and light. But in fact we know that this was actually an age of fierce contrasts, with a much more sombre side as well. It was not just in its silver flagons and flowing gowns that the Elizabethans' glittering new edition of the Renaissance imitated its Italian prototype. It seemed almost as though the English character itself had now borrowed from the fifteenth-century Tuscans a good deal more than their passion for poetry and music. The Elizabethans' extrovert love of flamboyant display is one conspicuous example that will spring to mind. Their swashbuckling 'braggadocio' is another. But there is also their dark streak of callousness, for in their lusts and cruelties they could sometimes prove as savage as the most ruthless of the 'condottieri'.

The first confident, carefree rapture of the Elizabethan Renaissance was soon succeeded by a more chastened mood, moreover, and a curious note of wistful sadness became apparent in the age which was to see Robert Burton write his great *Anatomy of Melancholy*. For many people, this was, in fact, a time of haunting uncertainty and doubt. They felt deep misgivings at the prodigious changes which occurred when the old order crumbled away during this bewildering transition from the medieval to the modern world. It was by no means easy, especially in a northern country with such an entirely different philosophy of life, to assimilate the Mediterranean Renaissance. Too many traditional ideas and values were called in question. The humanist approach, with its new confidence in man and the physical world, contained profoundly disturbing implications for the beliefs which had governed life in the past. And the ancient religious structure soon found itself seriously challenged by the spiritual renaissance of the Reformation and by revolutionary discoveries such as those of Galileo and Copernicus.

By the time that the Renaissance had at last reached the England of the Reformation, it had already become evident how difficult it must prove to reconcile the humanist ideal of man's greatness with the Church's teaching of human frailty and original sin. Spirits were increasingly troubled by the intellectual ferment of the age, and the men who cared most acutely about the perplexing new problems facing their generation were often besieged by self-doubts and anxieties, not so very different from those experienced by many people at the present day. Much of English art and literature at the beginning of the seventeenth century was overcast with a strain of introspective pessimism, which is equally symptomatic of our own Elizabethan age. The desperate scepticism of Shakespeare's darker tragedies and comedies reflects the inner tensions and conflicts from which it was by then so hard for a sensitive artist to escape. So do, for example, the paradoxes and ambiguities in the poetry of John Donne, who was to become a leading churchman and for whose divided spirit the reappraisals involved must have assumed a particularly agonizing significance.

The clash between the new humanism and his Christian faith presented difficulties of a special order for a staunch Puritan like Milton, even though his genius fortunately proved large enough to allow him to achieve a synthesis which could embrace his artistic as well as his religious convictions, 'to justify the ways of God to men'. Such efforts to work out an acceptable compromise between Christianity and the pagan aspects of the Renaissance could never be easy or painless. But it was not all loss: for they had the effect of stimulating the more thoughtful writers to reassess man's fundamental problems in relation to the universe. Their deep concern with the human predicament inspired them to create masterpieces of literature which were infinitely more than mere exercises in technical virtuosity.

But Milton, who was still writing as late as the 1660s, was to be the last of the outstanding European poets of the Renaissance. His achievement had only been possible because his Puritan austerity was tempered by a generous humanism learnt from the Mediterranean past. It had been against tremendous odds, however, that he succeeded in continuing the Renaissance traditions into a later age. For by the middle of the seventeenth century, it had become almost impossible to attain the kind of enlightened universality which enabled him to write as a member of the European literary community. In Italy herself the arts had acquired a different spirit under the pressures of the Counter-Reformation, and greatness had often yielded to grandiloquence. Italian civilization no longer reigned supreme in a Europe where intellectual horizons were once again being narrowed by nationalism and religious conflict. The horrors of the Thirty Years' War were a terrible reminder of the tragic split in Christendom left by the Reformation. Milton's England became the England of Cromwell and sectarian intolerance. The Puritan reaction, when the instinctive insularity of the middle classes reasserted itself against the Italianate cosmopolitanism of the 'Cavalieri', finally brought the Renaissance movement to a halt.

None the less, even the Puritans were seldom entirely insensitive to art, and the classics did not cease to be revered. The great light which had first been rekindled in Renaissance Italy was only temporarily obscured. It was never completely extinguished. For eighteenth-century Englishmen it would burn as brightly as ever before, and it has continued to illuminate our civilization down to the present day.

CHAPTER 3

THE AGE OF THE GRAND TOUR

A man who has not been in Italy is always conscious of an inferiority.

Dr Johnson

Eighteenth-century England was an extraordinary mixture of coarseness with a refinement which was mostly derived from Latin Europe. Although in other respects so complacently self-assured, the aristocratic élite who set the tone were well aware that there was still something parochial about English culture, and that it lagged behind the Italian and the French. In their anxiety to remedy their deficiencies, they travelled abroad in far larger numbers than ever in the past with the ambition of acquiring the sophistication of the more cosmopolitan societies of the continent. Even Dr Johnson, who epitomized the rugged insularity of the age, had no compunction in acknowledging that a great deal could be learnt from the older European civilizations, subscribing to the then fashionable opinion that the 'grand object of travelling is to see the shores of the Mediterranean'.

The English have always been a nation of travellers. We have seen that already in Elizabethan times they had been eager to visit Europe and especially Italy, where the Renaissance had reached its supreme achievement, in search of culture and refinement. In the early seventeenth century, Venice, for instance, had been one of their

45

favourite resorts. Not only did it lie next door to Padua, whose ancient university was widely patronized by English students. It had long possessed an exceptional political and commercial importance; and the oriental spice-trade with England had traditionally been carried in Venetian ships.

In the early years of the seventeenth century, moreover, a particular Venetian attraction was the English envoy, Sir Henry Wotton. The latter is seldom remembered today except for coining the aphorism, 'An Ambassador is an honest man, sent to lie abroad for the good of his country'. But in fact he was a remarkably gifted personality who became one of the first of this country's distinguished representatives abroad, and any young nobleman wishing to make a career in politics or diplomacy could do worse than spend some time in Venice observing his efforts to enlist the Republic's support for Protestant Europe. A visitor could equally learn a lot from Wotton about the new Italian culture. For the man whom Izaak Walton called 'a most dear Lover, and a most excellent Judge' of the arts was a knowledgeable collector, some of whose Italian pictures still hang on the walls of the Provost's Lodge at Eton. He was also a keen admirer of Palladio and author of the first English treatise on the aesthetics of architecture, a work which encouraged English appreciation of the Renaissance style soon to come into favour at home.

But only relatively few English families could afford the luxury of sending their sons to Italy at that period. Later in the seventeenth century, moreover, when the lessons of the Italian Renaissance had lost their first fascinating novelty and been absorbed, a reaction set in. Puritan England looked askance at Italy as a country of loose morals and the home of the Papacy. It was not Italy but France, whose prestige had been brought to its height by Louis XIV, which was in fashion by the reign of Charles II, himself a Francophil who had his French tailors and ordered his coronation robes from Paris. The English were dazzled by the magnificence of a monarchy whose grandeur recalled that of ancient Rome, and for a time they felt that it was French culture (which itself, however, owed a great deal to the Italian Renaissance and to the classics) that had most to teach them.

It was not until the beginning of the eighteenth century that Italy returned to favour once again. The homogeneous culture of the Augustan Age, the age of rule, reason and order, was based on the classics, which were accepted equally as a guide to life and as a hallmark of gentility. Every English gentleman was expected to take a cultivated interest in the Ancients, whose supremacy was seldom seriously questioned. The governing classes liked to picture themselves as spiritual heirs of Greece and, most of all, of Rome, and considered the ruins of the ancient civilizations almost as their own.

There consequently arose an intense curiosity about the lands of the classical past. For the English gentry it now became a fashionable ambition to see for themselves the country of the Roman historians and poets, on whom they had been brought up at school and whose names were household words in any educated family. In early Georgian times, Italy and her antiquities were appreciated, less for aesthetic reasons, than as illustrations of classical literature and history. It was only later in the century, when taste turned towards the Picturesque, that the English began to go to Italy in search of the landscapes of Claude and Poussin, rather than those hallowed by Virgil and Horace.

One of those who blazed the trail for the eighteenth-century wave of travellers was the author and Latin scholar, Joseph Addison. Nobody has written with greater enthusiasm of the lessons of antiquity and of the classical associations of the places which he visited. Since it was precisely those associations that then most interested the English, this helped to ensure the success of his *Remarks on Several Parts of Italy*, which many subsequent tourists used as a kind of guide-book. Addison explains in his preface that not the least of his 'entertainments' was to 'compare the natural face of the country with the Landskips that the poets have given us of it'. He provided some English translations of these poetic 'Landskips'; and such was the reverence for anything antique that no eyebrows seem to have been raised at infelicities like his rendering of Martial's verses on Capri and Tiberius:

> Who has not heard of Caprea's guilty shore,
> Polluted by the rank old Emperor?

When the worthy Addison had gone to Italy in 1700, it had been as bear-leader to two youths of good family. It was not long before it became a common practice for the aristocracy to despatch their offspring abroad for a year or two or often much longer, in order to complete their education with a leisurely continental tour under the supervision of some similarly respectable tutor. The principal purpose of sending a young man to see the world in this way was, in the words of an eighteenth-century prelate, that he should be 'polished into a general and universal humanity'; and it was generally agreed that this could be particularly well effected in Latin Europe and best of all in Italy. In those urbane surroundings and what Lord Chesterfield called 'the constant collision of good company', he could reasonably be expected to acquire sufficient cosmopolitan refinement to take the rough edge off his insular prejudices and fit him to play his part in polite society.

Thus was born the Grand Tour, the remarkable institution which did so much to bring to Georgian England the Italian influences that had such a fertilizing effect on British life and culture. A period of foreign travel came to be regarded as an almost indispensable complement to a gentleman's education. It was a sort of masculine initiation ceremony. Except in so far as it might sometimes be temporarily interrupted by war, this English social convention persisted during more than a century. It was not until after the Napoleonic wars that the Grand Tour entered into its final phase, before at last becoming submerged in mass tourism.

The tour developed into a fairly standardized affair as time went on. The main and most direct route for those heading South, after their stay in France or Switzerland, lay across the Alps. Before Napoleon built his military road over the Simplon, the Alpine crossing was considered a dangerous and disagreeable experience, demanding strong nerves. The final stage across the Mont Cenis Pass had to be negotiated in a primitive form of chair or wheelbarrow, through the kind of savage scenery which early eighteenth-century taste held in horror. Travellers were naturally heartily relieved, therefore, when they at last arrived safely in the civilized and ordered Italian landscape – what Peter Beckford called 'the long-wished-for plains of Italy'. Then, after a short halt at Turin or Milan, they would often first head for the bright lights of Venice.

Eighteenth-century Venice retained a flavour of the Orient, a city whose fascination still comes to life in the paintings of Longhi and Guardi or in the pages of Casanova. Apart from the famous courtesans, one of its most popular attractions was the sumptuous pageantry of its festivals and carnivals. The latter, lasting no less than six months every year, were unique in western Europe, and David Garrick wrote enthusiastically: 'I have seen here such sights I had no conception of but in Fairy land, and have seen the Visions of the Arabian Night realised by the Venetian regatta.' The English loved Venice, even though the place had evidently already acquired some of the characteristics of a modern tourist resort, and Gibbon, too serious-minded to be very susceptible to its pleasures and frivolities, remarked on 'its crowds and dearness' and 'shoals of English pouring in from every side'.

Florence was another almost obligatory stopping-place. The English visitors of the period, however, often seem to have found it rather a dull town, with 'no play, no opera, not even a puppet-show'; and the Florentines themselves, so Boswell complained, were 'very proud and very mercenary'. At the same time, there were, of course, all too many galleries which had to be visited. There the tourist would dutifully admire Michelangelo, Donatello and Benvenuto Cellini, although not the Botticellis, which were a much later discovery that we owed to Ruskin and Rossetti.

The prospect was brighter for those who had taken the precaution to arrive armed with a letter of introduction to the British envoy, Sir Horace Mann. He knew everyone worth knowing in Florence, for he spent so long there that he acquired a similar position to Wotton's in Venice a century before. The work of a diplomat at a small Italian court was seldom likely to be very arduous, and Gibbon records that Mann's 'most serious business was that of entertaining the English at his hospitable table'. Anybody as well-connected as Horace Walpole, for instance, could expect a warm reception from

Mann, who was delighted to launch him in local society. For Walpole, who formed a life-long friendship with his host, Florence was one of the more agreeable Italian cities – particularly at carnival time when, so he wrote, 'I have done nothing but slip out of my domino into bed, and out of bed into my domino.'

From Florence the tourists' trail led southwards, through 'sweet Siena', to Rome. Although then only a relatively small town of 150,000 inhabitants, it was far from lacking in social and artistic distractions. But for an age so passionately interested in the antique, the special fascination of the 'eternal city' lay in its classical associations and the stupendous Roman remains like the Colosseum, which were the visible foundations of Europe's history. Rome was revered as the city of the Caesars and of Virgil and Horace. Because it represented the very quintessence of antiquity, this was the Grand Tourists' Mecca – the one place in Italy which each of them must be able to say he had 'done' (an expression which would, incidentally, already be used by Lord Byron).

Most travellers pushed on as far as Naples, although they seldom ventured further south to Sicily or, still less, into the wilds of Greece, and it was only relatively late in the century that Paestum's splendid Doric temples were 'rediscovered'. Naples provided the natural culmination of the Grand Tour. This was not merely on account of its exceptional climate and the beauty of its setting. It was at that time the greatest city in Italy and the capital of the Kingdom of the Two Sicilies. Every visitor, whatever his tastes, could expect to find something to his liking in this busy metropolis which aspired to be regarded as 'the Paris of the South'.

The two most popular curiosities were Vesuvius and Pompeii, just as they are today. The 'terrible magnificence' of the volcano was a source of constant amazement: its eruptions in 1766 and 1778 created a tremendous impression, and British artists and scientists flocked to observe them. One enthusiastic student of these phenomena was Sir William Hamilton, the British envoy at Naples for nearly forty years during the latter part of the century. He published a number of learned treatises based on his observations at Vesuvius and Etna.

But above all he made a name for himself as an archaeologist, and the newly discovered Greek vases which he acquired went to form the nucleus of the British Museum's collections. (Hamilton was by no means the only British diplomat to go in for collecting; and the magnificent array of Canalettos bought by Joseph Smith, Consul and Resident at Venice, is now one of the glories of the British Royal Collection.)

The ancient villas on the Gulf of Naples, the 'sweet retirements of the most opulent and voluptuous Romans', as John Evelyn had called them, were also much admired. So was the Opera House, with its seven tiers of boxes, generally considered one of the most splendid sights in Italy. But a particular attraction of the San Carlo was the opportunity it provided for mixing with the local society, including sometimes even the royal family itself; and although Lady Mary Wortley Montagu might complain that the Neapolitan court, with its Spanish manners, was 'more barbarous than any of the ancient Goths', the average tourist was rarely so difficult to please.

Such were the highlights of the usual tour round Italy. The English milord, so long as he had a full purse and the right connections to secure the entrée into society, could hardly fail to find these Italian cities, with their easy pleasures, excellent places to amuse himself. A considerable proportion of those making the Grand Tour seem in fact to have done little or nothing else. A lot would, of course, depend on the tutors sent to chaperon them. Often English or Huguenot ecclesiastics attached to the family household, these were supposed to encourage the young men's studies and keep them out of mischief. But this was the most pleasure-loving of ages, and their charges were usually callow youths straight out of school or university, who idled away their time, preferring dissipation to education. Some people began indeed to feel that the British carried travelling a good deal too far, and Lady Hertford wrote from Italy in 1740: 'Most of our travelling youth neither improve themselves, nor credit their country.'

It may well be true that many of the Grand Tourists returned home little the wiser for their time abroad. Having had hardly any real contact with the ordinary inhabitants, they would probably have merely picked up a few foreign mannerisms and been confirmed in their insular prejudices. Fortunately, however, there were others, more intelligent or more mature, who were immensely enriched by their experiences. No doubt these only constituted the minority; but it is, of course, by no means uncommon for a new artistic movement (or even, for that matter, a political revolution) to be initiated by a very small minority indeed. Since these young men generally belonged to the ruling class of opulent Whig and Tory families who dominated politics, society and culture, lavishing their fortunes on splendid houses and works of art, the knowledge of Italian taste and civilization which they acquired could not fail to have far-reaching consequences for eighteenth-century Britain.

This was the age of the cultivated amateur, of connoisseurship and collecting. Smollett complained that the moment the English set foot in Italy 'they were seized with the ambition of becoming connoisseurs'. In any case, they were certainly overcome with a mania for buying up anything old they could lay their hands on, and one of Italy's attractions for them was that all kinds of antiques and *objets d'art* were so easy to come by. More than anything else, however, the tourists wanted Old Masters. 'All Europe was rummaged for pictures', says Defoe. But although the Italian collections were stripped, the English appetite was so insatiable that the supply could never keep abreast with the demand. A brisk trade in forgeries sprang up. 'Golden asses' was the name the Italians gave the young milords who could so easily be gulled into paying exorbitant prices for worthless fakes, and there was a saying that if the Colosseum had been portable the English would have taken it home with them (the fate that was, of course, actually to befall the Elgin Marbles).

There is, however, another side to the picture. To form a magnificent private collection now became as much of a status-symbol for noblemen as it had been for princes during the Renaissance; and the vast quantities of antiques, paintings and engravings shipped back from Italy did not consist entirely of fakes. They also included works of the first quality which would provide an important source of inspiration to British artists and architects – and ultimately even to the Romantic poets. Many of the returning tourists, moreover, did more than bring home Italian antiques and pictures. They also brought back with them Italian taste and an appreciation of the virtues of classicism which were destined to leaven English art and manners. It would often become their dearest ambition to Italianize the arts in England, with the object of rendering them less provincial.

The establishment of the Dilettanti Society in the 1730s, with Italian travel as a prerequisite for membership, put the seal of English social approval on the combination of connoisseurship and the 'giro' through Italy. Lord Shaftesbury had set the standards of the new generation when he preached that the art of Raphael and antiquity represented the acme of good taste and, as such, possessed a sort of moral sanction. Fortunately, however, it was not considered sufficient for a gentleman to take, or to affect to take, an interest in museum art: he was expected to patronize the living arts as well.

Italy had thus become generally acknowledged to be the best place to form the taste of any aspiring 'virtuoso' or 'dilettante' (both these favourite eighteenth-century expressions to describe a person possessed with 'virtú' or love and knowledge of works of art, were significantly themselves Italian). There he could prepare himself for his future role as patron of arts and letters in his own country. It was more often than not in Rome, where so many British artists went to study, that the young nobleman on his Grand Tour would first discover some painter or architect whose work particularly appealed to him. So might begin one of those associations between patron and artist which frequently proved so extraordinarily fruitful, as for instance in the case of Lord Burlington and William Kent.

An English author of the time described the three essential qualifications of a connoisseur to be money; the Grand Tour, including a visit to Rome; and a semblance of familiarity with Italian painting. He added that it was 'absolutely necessary, in order to paint an Englishman or an English landscape, that the artist should have studied the men and views of Italy'. It will later be seen how literally this recipe came to be applied. But the stalwart individualism of the English temperament – and individualism was a quality which was very far from lacking in eighteenth-century Englishmen – ensured that these foreign influences were absorbed into the native tradition and interpreted by artists and architects in terms of their own personal vision.

The Grand Tour, besides giving the British a taste for Italy's architecture and painting, which were to have so much influence on their own, also helped to stimulate their enthusiasm for yet another favourite form of Italian artistic expression. Italy had long been famous for her music, and this had, indeed, traditionally been one of her main attractions in English eyes. At the time of the Renaissance, Italian scholars had sought to reincarnate ancient Greek tragedy, with the result that Italy became the cradle of modern theatre and opera, both being art forms which are ultimately of Greek descent. Already in the seventeenth century Inigo Jones had elaborated the court masque on the basis of the Italian theatre; and subsequently Henry Purcell acclimatized the Italian style to the English tradition, acknowledging Italian music to be 'the best master' and advising English musicians to 'endeavour a just imitation of the most fam'd Italian Masters'.

The opera *Dido and Aeneas* was one of Purcell's greatest achievements, although in fact it was only given a single performance during his life-time at a school for young gentlewomen in Chelsea. But after his death in 1695 there were no English composers of comparable talent to continue with native opera. Foreign music had to fill the gap. The young Italophils who had been on the Grand Tour were eager to hear in England operas of the kind that had given them so much pleasure in Italy. In 1705, Vanbrugh's new theatre in the Haymarket was inaugurated with what appears to have been the first all-Italian spectacle in England. Italian opera quickly became the rage.

When Handel arrived here five years later after a period in Italy, he successfully exploited the demand for Italian music. Within a few weeks of reaching London he had composed his opera *Rinaldo*, and over the next thirty years he produced for Lord Burlington and other English patrons nearly forty more operas in the Italian manner. They were always sung in Italian and the best prima donnas and castrati (then a celebrated Italian speciality) were brought over from Italy to perform in them.

Eventually, however, some people began to feel that the fashionable cult of Italian operatics had been overdone, and John Gay took London by storm when, in 1728, he parodied them in his *Beggar's Opera*, a robustly English ballad-opera with a far wider popular appeal than the formal artificiality of the Italian genre. But the Italianate taste soon resumed its hold. Although Italian opera never again quite succeeded in repeating its first resounding triumphs, it retained an important place in London social life for generations, so that there was often more Italian opera to be heard here than in any other European capital. Serious musicians might sometimes have their reservations about its artistic merits. But even they recognized that Italy deserved to be considered as the main source of musical culture. Dr Charles Burney, for instance, who visited the country in the 1770s in order to gather material for his *General History of Music*, had no hesitation in describing the Italians as the most musical people in the world. He was particularly struck by the excellence of the Italian music schools and wanted to see them imitated in England.

So far as native English music is concerned, on the other hand, it would be idle to pretend that the eighteenth century was an outstanding period. With Handel and Italian music looming so large, our own musicians could hardly help being overshadowed. For all her contributions to the growing sophistication of musical appreciation here, Italy evidently failed to exercise a really effective creative influence on English music at this time. In Georgian England it was not music, but primarily the visual arts that were to be enriched by Mediterranean influences.

Literature requires some mention first, however. Whilst Italy's more modern writers usually failed to arouse any comparable interest, Latin literature, on the other hand, was held in extraordinary veneration in England, as was indeed every aspect of the Roman civilization from which the English Augustan age took its own ideals of dignity and restraint. In the eighteenth century, when even a plain country squire was expected not only to ride to hounds but also to know his

Horace, men of letters found it natural to look to the classics for their inspiration. English prose in the Baroque era was profoundly influenced by the Greco-Roman style. The ponderous sonority of Johnson or of Gibbon stems from their predilection for a Latin-derived vocabulary not dissimilar to Milton's. Rejoicing to call themselves 'Augustan' poets, Dryden and Pope translated Virgil and Homer, and the Latin satires provided them with models for their own. If authors such as these contributed so much to the new renaissance of classical culture, it was because, apart from imitating Latin forms and styles, they also sought to emulate the spiritual qualities which they found in Greek and Roman literature, morality and art.

This intense enthusiasm for the classical past prompted many other writers to follow in Addison's footsteps on a pilgrimage to the land of ancient Rome. Such people could seldom afford to travel in the luxurious fashion of aristocrats like Lord Burlington, who returned from his Grand Tour with no less than 878 pieces of baggage; and in his *Travels in France and Italy*, the novelist Tobias Smollett gives a lurid description of what he had to put up with from the Italian roads ('the very worst in the universe') and the filthiness of the verminous inns, which he describes as 'so abominably nasty' that even a common prisoner could expect better lodging in England. Travelling in Italy was in those days still very much of an adventure, generally uncomfortable, and sometimes (for there was always a chance of encountering 'banditti') a dangerous affair as well.

But some tourists were more philosophical than the cantankerous Smollett. For instance, another author, Oliver Goldsmith, who had to cover most of northern Italy on foot, was prepared to make a virtue of necessity, pointing out that those who travelled the hard way had a better opportunity of learning about the natives of the country than the rich who 'whirled through Europe in a post-chaise'. And whatever his tribulations, Smollett himself had, like so many others, fallen under the spell of the Mediterranean; he was in fact one of the first people to foresee the tourist possibilities of the Riviera (which was finally to be put on the map by Lord Brougham a century later). It is not inappropriate to find this author, whose philosophy and style derived so much from the Roman, returning to Italy to spend his last years there.

One writer who did a Grand Tour in the more orthodox fashion was James Boswell. But it was thanks to his detour to Corsica that he first made his reputation. His championship of the cause of General Paoli, who was leading an insurrection against the Genoese overlords of the island, appealed to the sentimental humanitarianism of the age. He became known in London as 'Corsica Boswell' and afterwards said that he had 'got upon a rock in Corsica and jumped into the middle of life'.

Boswell's experiences in the Latin South at an impressionable period in his youth influenced his ebullient personality, sharpening his taste and sensibilities. We can only regret that he never quite succeeded in persuading Dr Johnson to venture to Italy with him: for although Boswell's own travelogue is entertaining enough, we should find it more fascinating still to read the reactions of that most English of Englishmen to a Mediterranean exposure.

Another English author who gained a great deal from his foreign travels was Laurence Sterne, an exceptionally sensitive artist whose whole life was something of a Sentimental Journey. He was no longer very young by the time he got abroad, but his genius flowered late and he possessed the rare gift of retaining the receptivity of youth into middle age. His powers of observation were never more alert than during his tours in France and Italy. Bringing him romantic adventures which he could suitably embellish and embody in his writings, his travels helped to stimulate his emotions and lively sensibility for the composition of the two celebrated books, *Tristram Shandy* and *A Sentimental Journey through France and Italy*, which contributed so much to the refinement of the sentiments of the age.

But it is Gibbon's *Decline and Fall of the Roman Empire* which provides the most notable illustration of the way the Mediterranean world could inspire a great work of eighteenth-century English prose. Gibbon himself may be an example of the intellectual ascendancy of French culture, for his mind was cultivated in the French tradition. But the book which brought him fame was conceived in Rome;

ancient Italy and Greece were its subject matter; and it could only have been written by a man steeped in Greek and Latin literature, living in a society passionately concerned with the civilizations of antiquity.

The turning point in Gibbon's life came in October 1764. In the previous year he had joined the first rush of tourists to the continent after the Peace of Paris, at the beginning of the heyday of the Grand Tour. Amongst all the literary personalities who made the Tour, this earnest young man proved one of the most appreciative; 'every step I take in Italy', he wrote, 'I am more and more sensible of the obligation I have to my Father in allowing me to undertake the tour.' None was to owe a greater debt to Italy.

Rome was Gibbon's Mecca, what he called 'the great object of his pilgrimage', and he approached his goal in a state of high expectation and excitement. 'I can neither forget nor express', he was to record in his autobiography, 'the strong emotions which agitated my mind as I first approached and entered the *eternal city*.' For him, as for so many other travellers of his day, Rome was hallowed ground haunted by the ghosts of Romulus, Caesar and Cicero. After a sleepless night, he wandered amongst its ruins almost in a dream, musing on the transience of human greatness. 'Each memorable spot', he would later recall, 'where Romulus stood, or Tully spoke, or Caesar fell, was at once present to my eye; and several days of intoxication were lost or enjoyed before I could descend to a cool and minute investigation. . . .'

Thus the stage was set for one of those rare conjunctions of human genius and circumstances of time and place in which a masterpiece of art or literature may be conceived. Gibbon has left his own sober but evocative account of that enchanted Roman evening when he mounted the steps of the Capitol, and sat listening to the bare-footed friars intone their Christmas hymn in a church which had once been a pagan temple. It was then that the stupendous vision came to him of the vanished glories of ancient Rome, firing his imagination to attempt a description of the history of the great empire in its decline.

Gibbon's vast life-work, spanning over a thousand years and written in weighty Augustan cadences, forms an architectural whole as monumental and carefully proportioned as the ancient edifices which inspired it: even its imperfections stem largely from his Roman prejudices. The book was immensely influential at the time (Gibbon boasted that it was to be found 'on every table and on almost every toilet'). It still remains today a majestic memorial to the profoundly classical spirit of the Age of Reason.

Much more ordinary people, however, besides the heirs to great titles and estates, and the artists and the writers, began to take the fashionable road to Italy as the century wore on. Many belonged to the new middle class. More down-to-earth, they were inclined to be less easily impressed. They were even capable of reacting like the wife of a Scottish judge of the period on catching her first sight of Rome: 'I think', she remarked, 'it has a look of Aberdeen . . .'; and even Charles Dickens was later constrained to comment that Rome, seen from a distance, 'looked like LONDON!!!' But there were also, on the other hand, some very out of the ordinary person-alities, remarkable chiefly for their eccentricity, for the English were already discovering that they could afford to behave more uncon-ventionally abroad than they would ever dream of doing at home. It was not for nothing that Horace Walpole observed that what had struck him most on his Grand Tour was that 'there are no people as obviously mad as the English'.

One of the most notoriously unconventional was Frederick Hervey, Bishop of Derry and Earl of Bristol (who was also, incidentally, such a faithful patron of the best foreign hotels that a number of them still continue to call themselves 'the Bristol'). But shocking though his behaviour might often appear to his contemporaries, they could hardly help being fascinated by the bewildering diversity of this strange but exceptionally gifted character, who seemed equally in his element as a wit or rakish gallant, political intriguer, advocate of enlightened causes, fastidious connoisseur of the arts, and occasionally even in his proper role of prelate. He was – not least in his eccentricities – a typical product of his time; like so many others in that peripatetic age, he always remained an indefatigable traveller, and much of his refinement was the fruit of the years he spent in Italy.

Examples such as these may help to show how all kinds and conditions of Englishmen got caught up by the prevailing passion for foreign travel. The Grand Tour became, in fact, an essential feature of the eighteenth-century way of life. Thanks to its urbane influence on English tastes and behaviour, our ancestors were not all Squire Myttons. The best of them evolved into the sophisticated cosmopolitans to whom we owe the great British Age of Taste. Even when the predominant intellectual tendencies were French, Italy continued to be the main source of inspiration in art and manners. Much in British society and culture was Latinized as a result, with lasting consequences for our Anglo-Saxon civilization.

The tremendous impression made by the Grand Tour on the imagination of the age can still be seen from the great English houses, with their Mediterranean architecture and ornament, their galleries of Old Masters and British works in the Italian manner, and their setting in elegiac classical landscapes reminiscent of Claude or Poussin. These constitute an abiding monument to our Mediterranean heritage.

Such is the general background against which we can now consider some of the more striking of the countless contributions made by Italy and Greece to the development of the visual arts in Britain.

CHAPTER 4

ARCHITECTURE

The English, being essentially a practical people, have as a rule shown more disposition to excel in this branch of art, which can seldom be divorced from the practical problems of living, than they have in sculpture or even painting. Never has the national genius for fine domestic building been seen to better advantage than during the eighteenth century. And it is remarkable that, almost without exception, the outstanding British architects in that golden age of architecture learnt their craft in Italy. Their Italian training had a decisive effect upon their style, and they took their inspiration from the Mediterranean countries which had been the cradle of European architecture. The pattern was extraordinarily consistent. British architecture owed indeed so much to Italy and Greece that it can hardly be understood without some knowledge of the splendid buildings of Venetia, Rome and Athens.

But, as has been pointed out in a previous chapter, it was only very belatedly that the English felt the full impact of the Renaissance. Somewhat paradoxically, it was not in fact until Italy's own Renaissance architecture had fallen into decadence that British architects began to apply their genius to the reproduction of its past glories. During the Elizabethan age, when Italian culture had already begun to make so many other contributions to English civilization, this country's architecture remained surprisingly little affected by the stylistic revolution which had taken place in Renaissance Italy. The Tudors were capable of building fairy-tale palaces like Henry VIII's fabled Nonsuch, and many of the country houses of the period possess a charm and vigour of their own. But compared with the classical simplicity that was soon to follow, their style seems hybrid and provincial. Their besetting weakness was fussy over-elaboration, and their romantic fantasy belongs essentially to the Middle Ages.

Even as late as the beginning of the seventeenth century, the Renaissance still meant for English architects little more than the picturesque embellishment of what were really late medieval mansions, with ornament and decoration of a fresh naturalism which betrays its Italian origins. Earlier in this book, in the chapter on the Renaissance, various explanations have already been suggested for the curious insensitivity shown by English artists towards the new styles which had been invented in Italy. This is a phenomenon which appears to support the arguments of critics like Nikolaus Pevsner, who have maintained that the innate conservatism of the English temperament has repeatedly been reflected in English art. It does in fact seem to be the case that the latter has frequently needed the injection of foreign stylistic influences to rescue it from inertia. And this dependence on outside stimulus further emphasizes the indispensable nature of the Mediterranean contribution to the development of our civilization.

Fortunately, English architecture did not now have much longer to wait. By the Stuart times, interest in the rules of the classical and Renaissance styles was at last starting to increase here. Translations appeared of the Roman and Italian authorities like Vitruvius (who, in the first century AD, had laid down rules for the harmonious proportions of the Orders), Palladio and Vignola, and an English treatise on the subject was published by Sir Henry Wotton in 1624. Thus the ground was not entirely unprepared for the revolutionary transformation that began to overtake English architecture when it had been given a completely new direction by the mature Italianate manner evolved by Inigo Jones.

It was from the architecture of the Italian Renaissance that Jones acquired the conviction that a building must be designed as an organic whole, with a harmony and order based on exact mathematical proportions. Constructions of such complexity and sophistication could no longer, however, be left entirely in the hands of the master craftsmen who had been in charge of English building since medieval times. They now required a controlling mind and personality such as a man like Inigo Jones was able to provide; and it is Jones who is entitled to be regarded as the first English architect in the full modern sense of the term.

He had twice visited Italy as a young man at a time when the brilliant achievements of her Renaissance were still fresh and new. Andrea Palladio had only relatively recently completed the buildings in and around Vicenza which were destined to exercise such a remarkable fascination over successive generations of English architects. This sixteenth-century Paduan architect had had the original idea of grafting classical temple-fronts on to the façades of country houses (a highly improbable-sounding innovation which proved surprisingly effective, however); and the splendid country villas Palladio designed as summer places for the rich Venetians naturally had nothing whatever in common with the little suburban houses which go by that name today. Inspired by his ideas of the ancient Roman villas and temples and built on exact Vitruvian principles, they were urbane examples of Renaissance symmetry and harmony expressing the matchless serenity of classical grandeur.

It is easy to imagine what a tremendous impression the sight of so much magnificence must have produced on a sensitive young artist; and the time that Jones spent in Rome and northern Italy, assiduously studying the buildings and constantly consulting and annotating his copy of Palladio's *Quattro Libri dell'Architettura*, was decisive for the development of his style. He became the proverbial Italianate Englishman, ceaselessly nourishing his prodigious talents by drawing on his Italian experiences.

Before he went to Italy, Inigo Jones had already made a name for himself as a designer of court masques, and his introduction of movable scenery for this exceedingly popular form of Stuart entertainment shows his close study of Florentine precedents. He does not appear to have turned seriously to architecture until after his second Italian tour in 1614. No doubt he was impelled in this direction mainly by his discovery of Palladio. But there is another man who is surely entitled to a share of the credit for encouraging him in a career which would have such a momentous influence on the future of British architecture. For in Charles I he found the perfect patron. The King was a 'virtuoso', a connoisseur with tastes as Italianate as his own, and also with the courage to sponsor a completely novel style which must have seemed shockingly un-English to most of his subjects who had never seen anything remotely like it before.

Inigo Jones had been appointed Surveyor of the King's Works, and his most ambitious undertaking was to design the new Royal Palace at Whitehall. Only the Banqueting House was ever completed (in 1622); but it is a building which, as a work of art, invited comparison with the great masterpieces of the Italian Renaissance. Stylistically it was epoch-making: the clean lines of its elegant classical façade and the exploitation of the characteristic Palladian device of the 'double cube' show how well Jones had absorbed the Italian principles which inspired him. It marked the first complete break with the more parochial and essentially medieval style which had ruled in England hitherto. At the same time, it symbolized the philosophy of kingly power; but by an ironic coincidence, this building of revolutionary artistic significance, whose architect was the staunchest of royalists and a passionate believer in the divinity of kings, was soon to provide the setting for the revolutionary event which brought the political traditions of the Middle Ages to an end, for it was from its windows that King Charles stepped out on to the scaffold in 1649.

The output of Inigo Jones was never very extensive and although the Banqueting House still survives, much of his other work has disappeared. But enough remains to show the pervading Italian influence. There are rooms at Wilton reminiscent of the Pitti Palace, whilst Coleshill House in Berkshire, in the design of which he also had a hand, provides another classic example of the style of a Venetian villa. His scheme for the piazza at Covent Garden, with its Italianate arcades, seems to have been the first rational English attempt at town-planning since Roman times.

But it is perhaps the Queen's House at Greenwich which provides the most striking example of Jones's stylistic purity and command of classical form. He had begun work on this building very soon after his return from abroad, when the splendours of Italy were fresh in his memory, and its simple and perfectly balanced harmony breathes the serene spirit of Palladio. Even here, however, there was no slavish imitation, for this highly individual artist always gave his version of Palladianism a definite English character, 'solid, masculine and unaffected' – the words of Jones himself which epitomize the best traditions of British art.

The outbreak of the Civil War put a stop to new building and delayed the further Italianization of English architecture; and in any case the classical style of Inigo Jones was so alien and unfamiliar that other English architects were bound to hesitate to adopt it. Fortunately, however, an even more remarkable genius was very soon to emerge who would confirm the place that England had now begun to assume within the main traditions of European architecture. For Sir Christopher Wren, who only took up architecture after distinguishing himself as an inventor, scientist, mathematician and astronomer, was a man of such intellectual stature and protean talent that he would have been at home amongst the greatest Italians of the High Renaissance a hundred years before. He can indeed be regarded as the last of Europe's great Renaissance artists, in the same way as Milton was the last important European poet of the Renaissance age. England had had to wait an exceptionally long time before the Renaissance reached her but, in compensation, it was here that it enjoyed a final flowering. Wren was himself an inheritor of the Renaissance ideal of the 'universal man' – the brilliant 'all-rounder' who could excel at almost anything he chose with elegance and ease; and even as late as the following century, when this country's own architecture was becoming a perfect reflection of that of Renaissance Italy, there were to be a number of remarkably gifted English amateurs possessed with a comparable diversity of accomplishments.

Looking at the Palladian vistas of Greenwich or, better still, at the dome of St Paul's, whose splendour rivals the Roman St Peter's which inspired it, it is hard to believe that Wren, almost alone amongst the most prominent British architects of the period, failed to visit Italy. In fact, however, he never got further than Paris, where he did at least have the opportunity to meet Bernini, the great master of Italian Baroque, who allowed him a glimpse of his project for rebuilding the Louvre: 'Bernini's Design of the Louvre', he wrote, 'I would have given my Skin for, but the old reserv'd Italian gave me but a few Minutes View.'

But although Wren was mainly influenced by French classicism and never saw the architecture of Italy, he had studied the work of the Roman architects; and it was to Rome that his imagination instinctively turned when London had to be rebuilt after the Great Fire in 1666. To his logical mind this seemed a heaven-sent opportunity to create a noble capital on classical lines, and within a few days of the catastrophe he hurried to the king with an elaborate project for a spacious new city with broad piazzas and avenues 'contrived after the form of the Roman Forum'.

Wren's imaginative plan was eventually passed over. It was open to obvious practical objections, and it is easy to see now that it omitted to make sufficient allowances, not only for the vested interests involved, but also for English prejudices. Grandiose schemes of this kind have seldom been popular in a country where people suspect that, apart from the expense, they will probably impose a monotonous uniformity and deprive them of the informal irregularity which makes them feel most at home. The English have always been inclined to prefer picturesque individuality to the rational tidiness of Latin town-planning.

But even if Wren was not in the end allowed to create the Renaissance capital of his dreams, he could at least rebuild the city's churches, eighty of which had been destroyed by the flames. Here he once again showed his grasp of classical form in the ingenious variety of classical equivalents which he found for their Gothic spires. As befitted a man of the Renaissance, Wren naturally chose a dome for the greatest of them all; and after years of study and experiment, he finally brought to completion a masterpiece which, in its intellectual power and elaborate invention, ranks with the finest Cathedrals in the whole of Renaissance Europe.

In the second half of the seventeenth century, taste was turning to the Baroque, and a strong Baroque element can be detected in the work of Wren himself and sometimes already even in that of Inigo Jones. Reminiscent of styles frequently found in classical antiquity, Baroque had been invented in the Italy of the Counter-Reformation, and had by now become an international style which swept through all Europe. It is the style that can be found not only in the architecture of Vanbrugh and Hawksmoor, but also in the painting of Thornhill and Hogarth, the sculpture of Bushnell and Gibbons, the music of Purcell and the poetry of Dryden. During the whole of this period, however, France was constantly competing with Italy as the main source of English architectural inspiration, and in the 'grand siècle' the magnificence of Versailles inevitably struck men's imagination more than any Roman Baroque palace could hope to do. The foreign stylistic influences in the work of Wren's contemporaries and immediate successors often derived less therefore from Italy than from the classicism of the France of Louis XIV – or sometimes from the Netherlands of William of Orange.

But the English, with their puritan streak and instinctive preference for unobtrusive understatement, could not in the long run feel at ease with the exuberant flamboyance, the 'damned gusto', into which the Baroque style developed. Early in the eighteenth century, after the Tories had made way for the Whigs, there was a reaction against the grandiose architectural fashion which had produced buildings of such ponderous grandiloquence as Vanbrugh's gargantuan Blenheim or Castle Howard. A new and more restrained style emerged that was unambiguously based on Italian prototypes. This would be the beginning of a British age of noble classical architecture, dominated first by Lord Burlington and William Kent, and later by the brothers Adam, when the supremacy of Italian influences was seldom seriously challenged. The awareness of the classical tradition expressed itself not only in the architecture but in everything that was made at this time, ensuring a consistent standard of artistic design.

Eighteenth-century England was a paradise for the cultured amateur; and the new architectural mode was imposed by the advocacy and example of one of the most brilliant of the group of wealthy amateurs who were now becoming the arbiters of Georgian taste. This was the third Earl of Burlington, a prominent member of the Whig Establishment, Maecenas and prince of dilettanti. He became the high priest of the classical cult.

Like so many other rich young noblemen of his day, Lord Burlington had made the Grand Tour to Italy. It was there that his interest in the arts had first been seriously awakened and that he had fallen under the spell of the architecture of Palladio, much as Inigo Jones had done a century before him. He returned from his travels determined that English architecture must be reformed by abandoning the Baroque extravagance of Vanbrugh and Hawksmoor and reverting to the classical rule and order of the Renaissance.

We have grown so accustomed to Palladian architecture, much of which still surrounds us even today, that we tend to take it for granted and forget what an extremely odd phenomenon it represents in the history of art. For as Olive Cook has pointed out in her book on the English house, the Georgian style was in fact 'nothing more nor less than the imposition of the temple architecture of an extinct Mediterranean civilization upon the house design of a northern people'. But it becomes more easily explicable if we consider it against the background of the eighteenth century's consuming passion for the ancient world. This was the age when the ruling Whig oligarchy liked to imagine themselves heirs of the Romans, not only in their politics and morality but also in their art, and in their architecture they aspired to emulate the magnificence of classical antiquity. Their architectural ideal was based on the harmonious proportions of classical buildings; and any man of taste deemed it essential to be possessed with some knowledge of the Five Orders – Doric, Ionic, Corinthian, Tuscan and Composite.

For connoisseurs like Lord Burlington, the remains of the classical past constituted a standard of permanent values, hardly less than they had for Palladio himself. Many other Whig magnates were now returning from the Grand Tour fired with a similar enthusiasm for the architecture that they had discovered in Italy. They were eager to have houses which would advertise not only their wealth and station, but also the correctness of their taste, so that they wanted them to combine an impressive grandeur with a dignified restraint. In addition, they needed nobly proportioned rooms to show off the art collections they had amassed during their Italian travels. It was no great problem for the Earl to persuade his friends that the Palladian style would be ideally suitable to satisfy all these various requirements. The movement which he launched soon swept everything before it, and this Renaissance fashion became the accepted idiom for English architecture for a whole generation.

The school of Burlington believed it to be their mission to purify English architecture by going back to first principles and beginning again where Inigo Jones had left off. Even the great Wren had been too susceptible to French influences to meet with their complete approval. The earliest prophet of the new doctrine was Colen Campbell, whose writings proclaimed his Palladian enthusiasm and whose villa at Mereworth was inspired by Palladio's masterpiece, the Villa Capra, often called the 'Rotonda' (a building of such irresistible appeal to eighteenth-century Englishmen that they repeatedly took it as their model). But it was not Colen Campbell but William Kent who was destined to be Lord Burlington's most famous disciple and his chosen instrument to implement his cherished theories.

Burlington first became acquainted with Kent whilst he was making his Grand Tour. This versatile artist, who was nicknamed 'the Signor' by his English contemporaries, had been spending a considerable time in Rome, devoting himself to the study of painting. His true bent lay in other directions, however, and when Burlington paid his second visit to Italy with the avowed object of studying Palladio, he persuaded Kent to leave his Roman studio and accompany him back to England. It was thus that there began, in the year 1719, an historic partnership between patron and artist which was to create not only the English

Palladian style, but also a new conception of house-and-garden planning where the house was reduced from its dominant place in the landscape and became a less obtrusive part of the whole setting.

But Burlington was not merely a generous and enlightened patron. There is no need to go as far as York, where he designed the magnificent Assembly Rooms in the Palladian style, to see that he was a gifted amateur architect in his own right, even though he often relied on the help of William Kent and his flair for decoration. Burlington House in Piccadilly, now housing the Royal Academy, has long ago been altered almost out of recognition. But not everybody who hurries down the motorway to London airport may be aware that in the suburb of Chiswick the road passes alongside a quiet oasis where Burlington's own house, set in a park modelled on the principles of Claudian landscape painting, has been almost miraculously preserved, ranking among the most elegantly sophisticated of London's public treasures.

The typical Renaissance villa which Lord Burlington built himself there with William Kent's assistance after they had got back from Italy was, like Campbell's Mereworth, a free adaptation of Palladio's Villa Rotonda, having the same basic conception of a central room under a dome. But it contained a number of striking differences, such as the double flights of stairs at the entrances and the variations in the elevations. These innovations illustrate the resourcefulness of Burlington, who took ideas directly from Roman architecture as well as from Palladio, creating a synthesis that possesses an individuality of its own.

Lord Burlington evidently intended Chiswick House as an embodiment of his aesthetic ideals and as a place in which to house the works of art he had brought back from Italy, rather than as a house to live in. 'House!' exclaimed Lord Hervey, 'Do you call it a house? Why! It is too little to live in, and yet too large to hang to a watch.' Burlington himself would certainly have been unlikely to object when his noble friends aspired to something more grandly imposing than this relatively modest Palladian model. The monumental villas which he and Kent brought into fashion were symbols of their patrician age and established a clear link between British architecture and that of Italy. Not only were these houses based on Italian prototypes; sometimes they were even Italian-built, like Moor Park whose architect, Giacomo Leoni, belonged to Burlington's Palladian circle. Practically everything about them was Roman-inspired, whether it was their porticoed façades, their cornices and caryatids, their classical friezes, doorways, mantelpieces and coffered ceilings, or their magnificent gilded furniture.

One of the most palatial of these houses is the huge pile of Holkham in Norfolk where, behind an exterior of classical severity, there are rooms possessing an authentic Roman grandeur, and in its Great Hall the imagination of William Kent has succeeded in producing a superb expression of the spirit of antiquity. In the preceding chapter a good deal has already been said about the civilizing effects which the Grand Tour exerted on the English during the eighteenth century, by teaching them the arts of gracious living. The creator of this splendid house provides an example of the way in which this beneficial process operated in practice.

Thomas Coke, heir to vast properties and future Earl of Leicester, was one of the first of his generation to make the Tour. He had been a headstrong young lout of fifteen, chiefly interested in hunting and the bottle, when his guardians decided that the only hope was to pack him off abroad. Although this unprepossessing youth seemed singularly unpromising material, the experiment turned out astonishingly well. For in Italy, encouraged by a tutor from Cambridge who knew how best to handle him and foster his artistic interests, Coke discovered a taste for art and collecting and especially for architecture. Thanks to his six years on the continent, he developed into a typical product of that curious age: the English nobleman who combined a natural earthy coarseness with a genuine passion for the arts. Becoming one of the accomplished amateur architects of the time, he conceived the ambition to build himself a mansion of the utmost magnificence in the Renaissance style he had learnt to admire in Italy. Holkham owed a great deal to his friends Burlington and Kent (who had been his companion for much of his Tour), but a considerable share of the credit for this stupendous architectural achievement belongs to Lord Leicester himself.

It was of course only the very wealthy who could afford such palaces. 'Middling people' wanted 'middling houses', as Horace Walpole remarked in 1741. But the Palladian manner, although it did not really appear to lend itself to more modest houses, proved surprisingly adaptable. The decorous formality of the 'Georgian style', which we associate with the ordinary domestic architecture of the period, has a sense of harmony no less classical than the architecture of Palladio himself, and Palladian motifs are almost as common in the smaller houses as in the more famous mansions. Even in town architecture the English discovered a new use for Palladian grandeur. For the Palladian façade could be made to unite, in a single noble composition, the terrace houses that became such a prominent feature in Georgian urban planning. This was a device which was brilliantly exploited by the two Woods at Bath, where they were building on the actual ruins of classical antiquity, seeking to revive the ancient splendours of Aquae Sulis, as the Romans had called it.

The academic Palladian style survived well into the next century as a favourite mode of building for the rich and for public purposes. Its last great exponent was Sir William Chambers, best known, perhaps, as the architect of Somerset House. But its influence can still be detected in the work of Regency architects like John Nash, and even down to the present day, some relics of this Italianate manner can be found in the 'post-office Georgian' of municipal architecture. After the middle of the eighteenth century, however, its supremacy no longer went unchallenged. Kent and his followers had repeated the Palladian formula to the point of monotony. People were ready for something new and more exciting – or at any rate for some less stereotyped variation on the all-too-familiar Palladian theme. Alexander Pope was no doubt voicing the prevailing sentiment when he addressed his friend Lord Burlington with the gentle admonition:

> Yet shall, my Lord, your just, your noble rules,
> Fill half the land with imitating fools.

But although tastes were now beginning to change, the classical tradition still retained much of its old authority for the time being. In the eyes of an age which loved artistic good manners and had a horror of the 'barbaric', it continued to represent an impeccable 'correctness'. Robert Adam, the gifted and ambitious young Scot who launched the next architectural fashion, in fact accepted very much the same 'just and noble rules' as Lord Burlington had done himself. But he sought to interpret them in a more imaginative manner, shifting the emphasis away from the Renaissance and back to the Roman art which had been its original source of inspiration. He claimed to be nearer to the style of the ancients than the Palladians had been; for theirs had based itself on temples, whereas his own was, he maintained, derived from the domestic architecture of antiquity.

Like so many other architects of his day, including his main rival, James Wyatt, Adam studied in Rome, and it was Italy that prompted his principal innovations. Although he was too eclectic an artist to share the exclusive enthusiasm felt by the previous generation for Palladio, he did not entirely discard Palladianism in his own style. His particular interests, however, lay rather in the direction of the earlier Renaissance period and, most of all, the architecture and decoration of the ancient Romans themselves. Much more had become known about their domestic buildings since the excavations begun at Herculaneum in 1711 and at Pompeii in 1733. In Italy and also at Diocletian's palace at Spalato, Adam made numerous sketches which would provide him with ideas for his work in the future. It was, for example, his researches into the antique stucco decoration of the Romans that taught him how to use colour in his own ceilings.

Adam was captivated by the Roman achievement, and after his return to England in 1758, he drew on everything he had learnt from his Italian studies in order to create his own particular brand of classicism. The Palladians had created their version of the Roman villa. Robert Adam and his brothers were now to give us classical buildings of a rather softer and more poetical stamp. He prided himself on breaking away from Palladian rigidity and replacing it with a new sense of freedom and movement. His aim was, he said, to 'seize the beautiful spirit of Antiquity, and to transpose it, with novelty and variety'. With his shrewd perception of what would appeal to contemporary English taste, Adam in fact transcribed the massive plasticity of Roman architecture into a graceful and less substantial linear style of the kind that has generally been popular in this country.

At Syon and at Kedelston, where the central feature recalls a Roman triumphal arch, there are rooms on the grandest possible scale, worthy of the splendour of their Roman prototypes. But it was in his subtle and intricate designs for his interior decorations that Adam's inventiveness could express itself most brilliantly. Here it is the art of Pompeii, rather than that more commonly associated with ancient Rome itself, that seems to have been uppermost in his mind. He invented an imaginary 'Etruscan style', derived from the paintings on Greek vases, then generally supposed to be Etruscan; and for his celebrated 'Etruscan Room' at Osterley he elaborated a decorative scheme which includes motifs suggested by these ancient vases, by the school of Raphael and by Pompeian interiors.

Robert Adam has always had his detracters, and none of them has been more caustic than his own contemporary Horace Walpole, who sneered at what he called Adam's 'gingerbread and snippets'. Although in some of his later work he seems anxious to get away from the artificiality of his earlier manner, Adam himself would probably not have wished to lay claim to the masculine robustness of the Palladians – or certainly still less to the mock Gothic extravagances of Walpole's own house at Strawberry Hill. It might be a fair criticism to say that he sometimes only succeeded in achieving mere ornateness when straining after antique grandeur, and he could on occasion be capable of an exquisite frivolity which has inevitably exposed him to charges of superficiality. None the less, Italy had taught this extraordinarily versatile genius both nobility of conception and elegance of detail. It was his peculiar gift of combining the two together which makes an Adam house such an enchanting symphony of grace and delicacy, lightness and fantasy.

Despite the immense popularity which his style enjoyed, Adam never dominated the English architectural scene to quite the same extent as the Palladians had done a generation before. In the second half of the eighteenth century, the critical new spirit abroad in Europe found its reflection in the British attitude to the arts. The homogeneity of English architecture was already starting to disintegrate. After the long Palladian reign, the classical convention itself began to pall and no longer found universal acceptance. The challenge from the Rococo had, it is true, left less of a mark on English architecture than on the decorative arts, and the competition from the Gothic Revival had not yet assumed the formidable proportions which it would in the future. However, the cult of the Picturesque, which had at first been mainly confined to landscape gardening, was now making its influence felt in other fields as well. In architecture it admitted irregularity of design, and it was not long before John Nash would be experimenting with houses as picturesquely irregular as the architectural fantasies in Claude's paintings. So the door had been opened to stylistic eccentricities which were the very antithesis of the classical ideal. This was, in fact, the dawn of the new era of Romanticism.

But although there were now a bewildering variety of fresh currents of taste which deprived it of the virtual monopoly it had previously enjoyed, the classical style was not yet by any means a spent force. A European movement had emerged which gave it a further lease of life in the guise of 'neo-classicism'. The latter was to prove a highly complex and somewhat confusing phenomenon, not least because it overlapped with the beginnings of the Romantic Movement, both in time and in sentiment; and many of the artists who now looked back so nostalgically to the vanished glories of an idealized classical past were themselves unconscious romantics.

But the origins of the new movement are not particularly difficult to explain. In essence, neo-classicism was yet another manifestation of the same eighteenth-century passion for antiquity that had earlier given birth to Palladianism. Nowhere in Europe did this antiquarian enthusiasm exercise a more powerful influence than in this country, and the British played a prominent part in developing the new style.

Soon, they had even introduced it as far afield as Russia, where neo-classicism was used with taste and elegance by Charles Cameron in the palaces at Tsarskoe Selo and Pavlovsk.

The archaeological discoveries at Herculaneum and Pompeii earlier in the century had stimulated a tremendous surge of interest in the Roman achievement. Here, so it seemed, was confirmation of the pre-eminence of the ancient civilization on which the Georgians sought to base their own culture. Artists were encouraged in their reaction against the exuberance of the Baroque, and prompted to return to the serene simplicity of classical art.

By the middle of the eighteenth century the time was therefore ripe for yet a further variation on the well-worn classical theme. Not surprisingly, this was prone to the over-refinement which is so often associated with the concluding phases in the evolution of any artistic style. The neo-classical seldom warms the heart. But although lacking the virile simplicity and vigour of earlier versions of the classical, neo-classicism sometimes possessed an exquisite delicacy. Often cold and correct, it could also be capable of an almost feminine prettiness, well calculated to appeal to the craving for elegance of the new middle class which the Industrial Revolution was bringing into existence. Its lofty idealism and highly serious moral tone, so different from the frivolities of the Rococo, also helped it to gain bourgeois approval.

Neo-classicism was amongst the most important of the manifold ingredients which went into the making of the very personal style of Robert Adam himself. But the influence of this new aesthetic approach was far from being confined only to architecture. In the second half of the eighteenth and the beginning of the nineteenth centuries, the 'antique taste' extended to all the arts. It did not merely inspire sculptors to emulate the Italian Canova in imitating classical models, and artists like Gavin Hamilton and Benjamin West to paint classical and historical subjects in the 'grand style' which Reynolds preached but seldom himself practised. Romney is an example of a painter who did not finally become engrossed in fashionable portraiture until after he had gone through a neo-classical period. Even Blake, although his mystical vision could not be compatible with the academic theories of neo-classicism for very long, passed through a similar phase and invoked the authority of Greek art for his emphasis on outline – 'the bounding line' which he once called 'the great and golden rule of art, as well as of life'.

In interior decoration neo-classicism provided the perfect complement to the architecture of the Adam period. The Italian artists working in England were in great demand to paint mural decorations in the fashionable new manner. They included Cipriani and Zucchi, the husband of Angelica Kauffmann, who had been brought over by Adam to work on his interiors; and although none of these Italians was a painter of the first order, much of their work possesses the same element of delightful fantasy as can often be found in that of the Italian, or Italian-trained, plasterers who were responsible for so many minor masterpieces in eighteenth-century English houses.

Neo-classical influences are equally apparent in the furniture of the time. The ornate and sumptuous opulence of William Kent now gave way to a lighter and more fastidious style, where every detail contributes to create an impression of unselfconscious domestic grandeur. Whereas Kent had taken his inspiration from the magnificence of Roman and Venetian Baroque, Adam and Chippendale preferred a more austere elegance deriving from classical antiquity.

The influence of the new taste was all-pervading. Even fashions in dress were affected. Next to the architecture of Robert Adam, however, it is probably the splendid simplicity of the pottery of Josiah Wedgwood which is now the best known example of English neo-classicism. His copies and adaptations of antique Greek urns and vases were much sought after, playing an important part in promoting neo-Grecian tendencies in the arts. Like Adam, he shared the prevailing misapprehension that the antiquities which had recently been discovered in southern Italy were of Etruscan origin, so that when he rebuilt his factory in 1770 he christened it 'Etruria'. It was only afterwards, when he had discovered that these objects were in fact not Etruscan but Greek, that Wedgwood came to realize that Greece could offer the nobler source of inspiration.

But it is architecture which provides the most illuminating illustration of this all-embracing movement, both in its complexity and in its achievements. One complicating factor is the difficulty of disentangling its two main strands, the Greek and the Roman. In the second half of the eighteenth century, some people fervently believed that ancient Greece was the civilization most deserving of imitation. Others, on the contrary, were equally passionately convinced that Rome offered the best model. In this prolonged and acrimonious dispute it was at first the enthusiasts for Rome who had the upper hand. They could point to eloquent interpreters of Roman architecture not only in Robert Adam but in William Chambers, the most prominent official architect of the time, who criticized the Greek style as 'ridiculously barbaric'.

More important still, Roman art and architecture started with the advantage of having been the traditional source of artistic inspiration over so many centuries. They were at the time far better known than the Greek. Rome was the greatest surviving city of antiquity and the school for artists from all over western Europe. Its ancient ruins surrounded any visitor on the Grand Tour. A wealth of antique Roman statuary was available for him to study in the Vatican galleries, and he might follow the fashion by acquiring specimens for a collection of his own. Even those who had never been to Italy, moreover, were now able to derive a superb impression of the Roman past at its most magnificent from the breathtaking grandeur of the visions of Adam's Venetian friend Piranesi, whose splendid etchings found their way into so many eighteenth-century libraries.

English ideas of Greece, on the other hand, were still much more imprecise. As compared with the living reality of ancient Rome, Hellas was little more than a misty dream. In a remote way, it had always been honoured as the cradle of Europe's civilization, and the Homeric legend had survived. But few travellers were as yet prepared to brave the dangers and discomforts of the backward Turkish province that Greece had long since become, and Greek art continued to remain virtually unknown except through inferior Roman copies. It was not until the 1760s that the English could at last begin to form a clearer conception of the Greek architectural achievement thanks to the publication of the *Antiquities of Athens* by Stuart and Revett, who had been sent out to Greece by the Dilettanti Society.

The partisans of Greece now found an influential ally in the German scholar, Johann Winckelmann. He was the great theoretician of the classical argument. The magnificent rhetoric of his prose created an idealized Greece – the vision of a land of demigods and heroes which has haunted the European imagination ever since. Firmly convinced of the fundamental mediocrity of Roman art, he was an impassioned advocate of the ultimate authority of the art of classical Greece. He taught his age to revere it as the embodiment of the Greek spirit, preaching that the modern artist could learn more by imitating its 'noble simplicity' than by copying nature itself, and that its serenity might still help mankind to lead happier lives.

By the 1790s the protracted 'battle of the styles' was turning decisively against the Roman and in favour of the Greek, and the century when Rome had set the tone for so much in British artistic as well as political and moral ideals ended on a Grecian note. And even at the present day, when so many of our long-cherished beliefs have been discarded, it seldom occurs to us to question that Greek art possesses a unique quality of the kind which Winckelmann so eloquently claimed for it.

The earliest Greek Revival building anywhere in Europe was the miniature Doric temple which 'Athenian' Stuart erected for Lord Lyttleton at Hagley in 1758. But it would be another fifty years before his message of Grecian purity and simplicity won general acceptance. It was not until 1808 that Smirke gave London its first Doric building when he reconstructed the theatre at Covent Garden with a Greek portico. From that date the Grecian style was finally accepted as the yard-stick of architectural orthodoxy and 'Grecian Gusto' became the rage.

The decisive triumph of this style was precipitated by an event which enormously stimulated British interest in Greek civilization. At the beginning of the nineteenth century little had been known about other forms of Greek art apart from architecture. It was only when the British government acquired the Parthenon marbles from Lord

Elgin in 1816 that, for the first time in western Europe, an important collection of Greek sculpture of the best classical period was at last put on public exhibition. The impact of the marbles was tremendous, not least on literature, as can be seen, for instance, from the poetry of Keats. They moved the latter's friend, the painter Benjamin Haydon, to an enthusiastic outburst: 'I felt as if a divine truth had blazed inwardly upon my mind and I knew that they would at last rouse the art of Europe from its slumber in the darkness.'

But many neo-classical artists were shocked to discover that these masterpieces of Phidias revealed an art of a naturalism very different from their own preconceived ideas. Most British sculptors seem in fact to have found them too big a challenge, preferring to cling to the bland and insipid Hellenistic style of which Canova was the acknowledged master. The spurious elegance of neo-classicism retained its immense popularity, and statues in smooth white marble remained a favourite decoration for gentlemen's conservatories well into Victorian times. Nor do the friezes appear to have had much direct influence on architecture, although they clearly inspired the friezes on Decimus Burton's screens at Hyde Park Corner and at the Athenaeum. But whilst they failed to lead to the new English Renaissance for which some people had hoped, there is no doubt that the Elgin Marbles had an effect on the general taste, and by enhancing the prestige of the antique they encouraged architects to proceed with building in the Greek Revival style.

The newly acquired marbles from the Acropolis soon needed a Greek temple in which to house them, so Sir Robert Smirke was commissioned to build the British Museum, whose interminable colonnades of giant Ionic pillars aspire to rival the Parthenon. William Wilkins, who had a passion for Greek temples, used an equally classical style for the National Gallery, designing a Grecian portico to take the columns from Carlton House, which had earlier been metamorphosed by Henry Holland in a strictly neo-classical manner.

But neither of these architects possessed the power to infuse their work with the true spirit of Greek architecture. In fact, it is not in London but in Edinburgh that are to be found the most splendid series of public buildings in the classical style. The design of the New Town had been begun by Robert Adam towards the end of the previous century, and after the Napoleonic wars so much neo-classical architecture was introduced that the inhabitants spoke of it as a modern Athens. Edinburgh was transformed into a classical city, as nobly laid-out as any in Europe, a serene and evocative monument to the architectural achievement of the Greek Revival.

Despite the fashionable enthusiasm for 'all things chaste and Greek', Grecian neo-classicism was now by no means alone in the field, however. There was a hotchpotch of rival styles during the first half of the nineteenth century. Sir John Soane, for instance, is another example of the English architects with a Roman training, and he was sometimes called 'the last of the Romans'. But he became converted to the Greek, and by the time he rebuilt the Bank of England he had developed a highly personal idiom which borrowed as much from Greece as from Rome. On occasions he would dabble in the Gothic as well. Yet another prolific architect with a wide variety of hybrid styles was Jeffry Wyatt, who was knighted for his work at Windsor Castle and took the resounding title of Sir Jeffry Wyatville.

John Nash provides an even better illustration of the stylistic confusion which prevailed. The 'Regency style', which was largely his creation, was essentially classical, but Nash himself was an eclectic architect who also worked with an equally plausible facility in the Gothic and the Picturesque. Amongst all these different trends of taste, it was, however, the cult of the Picturesque which seems to have been the most fundamental influence in this high summer of Romanticism.

This is, indeed, the case with Nash himself. It was thanks to his intense feeling for scenic effects that he became the brilliant town-planner who aspired to transform the face of London as splendidly as the landscape-designers had transformed the English countryside. His vision of Regent Street would have made it the finest thoroughfare in Europe. His classical, Doric-pillared terraces and crescents at Regent's Park may be open to criticism from the purely architectural point of view. But their urbane nobility can hardly be disputed, and regarded as the exercise in the Picturesque which was evidently Nash's own main intention, their panache is triumphantly successful. Seen as a townscape, the stupendous panorama is incomparably effective.

A new Italianate fashion had meanwhile been launched in the 1830s by Charles Barry, who had toured Italy soon after the end of the Napoleonic wars and come back with an enthusiasm for her 'palazzi'. He introduced this style into London street architecture with his designs for the Travellers' Club and the Reform. This was the heyday of club building and the whole of London's clubland is a monument to the English taste for the classical. Thackeray once described it: 'Yonder are the Martium [the United Services Club] and the Palladium [the Athenaeum]. Next to the Palladium is the elegant Viatorium [the Travellers']. By its side is the massive Reformatorium [the Reform], and the Ultratorium [the Carlton] rears its granite columns beyond.'

By this time, however, the long classical era in the history of British architecture was at last drawing to its close. Signs of debility had already been apparent in the excessive refinement of neo-classicism and the theatrical stucco buildings of John Nash's Palladian Picturesque. Gothic, the style which had once been ousted by the classical and had at one time appeared to be virtually moribund, now took its revenge. To the Victorians, it was evocative of the medieval past which had so much appeal to their sentimental romanticism, whereas classicism seemed to them frigid and artificial in its impersonal formality. These feelings were crystallized by Pugin's powerfully reasoned advocacy of the Gothic Revival. He encouraged the idea that this represented a return to a Christian and genuinely native style (oblivious of the fact that the Gothic had originally come to us from France), after the 'aberrations' of the pagan and alien classical tradition. For a time the new movement also derived support from the persuasive prose of John Ruskin, the great arbiter of Victorian taste and the impassioned champion of Venetian Gothic, for whom the Gothic style was not merely supremely beautiful but the spiritual expression of an age of faith.

Neo-Gothic had received the accolade of official recognition when the style was chosen for the rebuilding of the Houses of Parliament in the 1830s. But even the new Goths did not disdain the gentlemanly rules of classical proportion; and Barry and Pugin, who collaborated on the project, worked out an appropriately English compromise. For although the construction is neo-Perpendicular in detail and ornament, it is still basically classical in the symmetry of its design. Pugin himself ruefully complained that the building had finally turned out 'all Grecian'.

There now followed a period when Gothic, Greek and Italian styles co-existed happily, engendering many other curious hybrids. It was not until the middle of the century, when England experienced what Roger Fry once called a tragic change to 'Philistinism, Puritanism and gross vulgarity', that the Gothic Revival finally won the day. But even afterwards the Gothic supremacy did not go entirely unchallenged. As late as 1857, Lord Palmerston rejected Sir George Gilbert Scott's neo-Gothic plans for the Foreign Office in favour of a design on Renaissance lines. It can scarcely be claimed that the building which this produced is in itself a thing of great beauty. But seen from across the lake in Nash's St James's Park, and flanked by the Palladian façade of William Kent's Horse Guards, the view unites architecture and landscape with a serene magic evocative of those paintings of Claude which had so long captivated the English imagination.

Because it still seemed to contain an element of matchless dignity and timelessness, the classical style was in fact never completely supplanted by the neo-Gothic as the approved style for public and official buildings. Familiar to every Londoner is the extraordinary juxtaposition of the Albert Memorial (once considered 'beyond question the finest monumental structure in Europe'), which is mock Gothic at its most extravagant, and the Albert Hall, built shortly afterwards in a diametrically contrasting idiom evidently deriving from the Roman Colosseum. Even in the present century the time-honoured classical style has frequently continued to be chosen as particularly suitable for edifices which were supposed to create an impression of pomp and circumstance. The results, although possibly no worse than the excesses perpetrated in the name of the Gothic Revival, have often been little short of disastrous. Instead of being honeyed by the sunshine of the South, these reproductions of Roman civic buildings are usually grimy and smoke-darkened. Lacking the uplifting vitality of their Mediterranean prototypes, they are seldom likely to lighten the hearts of those seeing them today.

But there have also occasionally been less deplorable examples. When the modern capital of India was laid out at New Delhi in 1912, the classical style was used effectively by Sir Herbert Baker and Sir Edwin Lutyens to create a supreme expression of triumphant imperialism such as the Romans themselves might have envied. In his country houses too, Lutyens's brilliant talents could strike a spark from its dying embers. For Lutyens, Palladio was the 'high game' of supreme importance to any serious architect, and his own maturer style he called 'Wrenaissance'. But he was the last British architect of distinction to work in a convention which had by then become petrified and lifeless; and despite the exceptional elegance of his restatement of the well-worn classical themes, he often leaves an impression of artificiality and pastiche.

Even in the architectural revolution of the present time the old traditions have still not been altogether forgotten. Interest in the study of English classical architecture has recently been reviving, and some critics even believe that they have discovered a relationship between the modern international style and the cubic simplicity and austere lack of ornamentation of Palladianism. But in this day and age, architecture finds itself confronted with problems which bear so little resemblance to those of former periods that the precepts of the past no longer appear to have more than a very limited relevance. New constructional materials and new ways of handling space are increasingly the centre of attention; function, rather than appearance, is the order of the day, and the engineer has been encroaching on what used to be regarded as the architect's preserve. Under the pressure of the population explosion, the emphasis has shifted from houses to 'housing'. One consequence has been the vast and hideous spread of suburbia, where countless little villas continue to be erected in a pathetic parody of Georgian gentility.

14 The Etruscan Room
at Osterley Park,
Middlesex (see page 74)

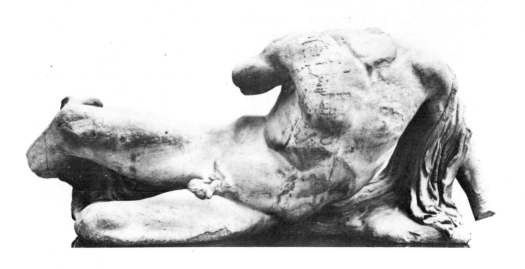

15 The disturbing naturalism of the Elgin Marbles *(see page 80)*

16 The British Museum, with its forest of Greek columns (*see page 80*)

17　The Reform Club, an example of Charles Barry's taste for the Roman (*see page 82*)

18 Pompeo Batoni's group of English tourists in Rome, about 1750 (*see page 95*)

19   Reynolds's *Commodore Keppel (see page 91)*

20 *Poussin's Landscape
in the Roman Campagna (see
page 98)*

Modern architecture can at its best possess impressive and refreshingly exciting qualities which make it infinitely more satisfying than any nostalgic attempts to reproduce yet once again the dead styles of the past. But faced with the utilitarian uniformity of so many of the mass-produced buildings of today, depersonalized box-like structures which seem all theory and no soul, we can hardly help regretting earlier ages when there were generally accepted standards of taste and a coherent national style able to engender such an abundance of grace and beauty. From that point of view the English eighteenth century was unsurpassed. Great country houses of the same nobility and refinement are never likely to be built again in socialistic times like these, and those that still survive are monuments to a very different way of life. They could only have been produced by a society which attached more importance to grandeur and ostentation than to comfortable living, but set most store of all by the Rules of Taste.

These Italianate villas may look a little incongruous under our grey English skies. Their cool, spacious rooms are provided with an elaborate system of cross-draughts which had originally been specifically designed against the heat of the Venetian summer. Already Alexander Pope had twitted the English Palladians with being 'proud to catch cold at a Venetian door', and it would be idle to pretend that these houses are really suited to this northern climate. But it would equally be impossible to deny that they rank amongst the most magnificent to be found anywhere in Europe. Like so much in British architecture, which, next to the written word, is this country's greatest contribution to the common patrimony of western culture, their captivating splendour shows the memorable achievements of which our native genius could be capable when it turned to the Mediterranean world for its inspiration.

CHAPTER 5

PAINTING

I could exhibit a long catalogue of soldiers, statesmen, orators,
mathematicians, philosophers, etc. which do honour to our country.
But as I confine myself to the arts, I will only instance Inigo Jones,
Shakespear and Milton, and leave them to seat themselves at the
table of fame amongst the most illustrious of the ancients. A time
may come when future writers may be able to add the name of an
English painter. . . .

Jonathan Richardson

At the beginning of the eighteenth century when Richardson was
writing, painting was still something of a Cinderella of the arts in
England. It is true that it had some earlier accomplishments to its
credit. Like our embroideries, English illuminated manuscripts, at
any rate, had gained an international reputation in medieval times.
But this earlier artistic tradition came to an end around the year
1400, and there followed nearly three centuries during which not a
single first-class painter was born in Britain. Art-lovers like Richardson
inevitably began to wonder whether England would ever be able to
equal the rest of Europe, where so many brilliant painters had already
appeared long before.

We have seen that even the golden age of Queen Elizabeth I, when
this country was creating some of the finest of the world's poetry, as
well as so much delightful music, proved relatively barren in painting;

87

and so far as native-born painters were concerned, it was little better during the following century, rich though that was in noble English architecture. For an extraordinarily long time it seemed as if the revolution in painting, which had been one of the most splendid achievements of the Italian Renaissance, would virtually pass England by. It was not until well on into the eighteenth century, after English artists had assimilated the lessons which Italy could teach them, that a national school of painting at last reached maturity, and the English started to produce good painters of their own instead of merely importing them. The great age in the history of British painting which then began lasted for approximately one hundred years, until the death of Turner in 1851, and during the whole of that period the influence of Italy on British artists was usually paramount.

It is tempting to speculate whether it would have been necessary to wait quite so long for the flowering of British painting if there had been closer contact with Italian art before. But Holbein, Rubens, Van Dyck, Lely and Kneller, the foreigners working in England who domi-nated the scene, were none of them from southern Europe, so that for centuries the English were obliged to learn about Italian painting mainly at second hand. It proved a painfully slow process which first started in Tudor times. Holbein, the great German artist of the northern humanist movement who enjoyed the favour of Henry VIII, possessed an instinctive sympathy with the spirit of the Renaissance; and some Italian elements can already be detected in the work of Nicholas Hilliard, who ranks amongst the most lyrical of the Elizabethan miniaturists.

British taste received a more significant impetus in the Italian direction under the first Stuarts, however, when it became fashionable to be a 'virtuoso' or connoisseur. Although Rubens spent only a few months in this country, his painting in Inigo Jones's Banqueting House at Whitehall was the beginning of an English tradition of Baroque based on Veronese and the great Venetians. Influences of a similar kind reached us through Van Dyck (whose name we Anglicized as Sir Anthony Vandyke). Before his appointment as court painter to Charles I, this Flemish artist had absorbed a great deal from Italy during the years which he spent in Venice studying Titian and Giorgione. He brought something of the nobility of the Venetian portraits into our own traditions of portraiture, so that Italian dignity and refinement became qualities sought after by successive generations of English painters.

The King who had encouraged Rubens and Van Dyck to come here possessed a genuine love and knowledge of Italian art. He patronized Italian painters like Gentileschi and commissioned the famous Roman sculptor Bernini to model his bust. Charles I was also almost the first of the great English collectors of Renaissance Old Masters. His new vision of the world might, indeed, have made this country the artistic centre of Europe. Or so it had briefly seemed, until the Puritan revolution led to the dispersal of his great collection and put an end to all such dreams.

The period that followed, when England was ruled first by the Puritans and then by Francophil monarchs, could hardly be expected to be conducive to the further spread of Italian influences. Nor, in fact, were the initial results particularly happy when closer contacts with Italian art were at last established in the final quarter of the seventeenth century. Unfortunately, Italian Baroque, which had by then gained general acceptance as the European style, only reached England in an attenuated decorative version. Characteristic examples can be seen at Windsor and Hampton Court, where Antonio Verrio painted his exuberant ceilings. This Neapolitan was the first Italian painter to make his mark in England, but nowadays he is considered so second-rate that it is difficult to account for his enormous popularity in his day except as a reflection of the poverty of English taste at that time.

Some improvement occurred when other artists arrived from Italy a generation later. The work of Venetians such as Pellegrini and the Ricci had at least more elegance than Verrio's, and proved itself very suitable for decorating the splendid new buildings now springing up here. Under their influence, British painters grew relatively proficient in the Italian Baroque style. Sir James Thornhill, who decorated the Painted Hall at Greenwich, often described as the grandest painted room in Britain, was a gifted representative of this more encouraging trend. Both he and Pellegrini had a hand in founding London's first academy of painting in 1711, which was planned to be on similar lines to the artistic academies which had long been flourishing in Italy.

British painters were by this time becoming increasingly familiar with the work of the great Italian masters. Before the middle of the century British art at last began to catch up with the continental tradition and to come into its own. Not only painting, but even sculpture, still conspicuous for quantity rather than quality, benefited from the English interest in foreign art and antiquities which had been stimulated by the Grand Tour. The numerous portraits of Augustan gentlemen in antique costume testify to the new taste; and after the death of Kneller there was an interval when the best British portraiture took the form of sculptured busts in the classical manner which came into vogue with the Whig nobility who liked to fancy themselves the embodiment of the republican virtues of ancient Rome.

But much better things were now at hand. There finally emerged a painter of genius who was also unambiguously English. William Hogarth was indeed in many ways the most insular of artists. But although his individuality and nationalism led him to ridicule the blind veneration of Old Masters which had by then already become the fashion, he did not hesitate to pillage them for his own compositions. And when he eventually published his artistic theories in his *Analysis of Beauty* in 1753, it was evident that these were in fact very largely based on those of the Italians.

Hogarth had, moreover, ambitions to win fame as a history painter, following in the footsteps of his father-in-law, Sir James Thornhill. In some of his larger works, such as his excursion into fresco to decorate St Bartholomew's Hospital in London, he even attempted the Italian Grand Manner on his own account. For an artist who was essentially a satirical genre painter, such experiments were too out of character to meet with any great success, and Reynolds was not alone in deploring them as 'very imprudent and presumptuous'. But it would be fair to add that in one important instance at any rate, Hogarth managed to achieve a dignity which clearly derived from the

European style. For in his portrait of Captain Coram he produced a masterpiece; and this splendid painting was instrumental in helping his contemporaries to escape from the baneful influence of the stereotyped Kneller convention.

Although Hogarth has often been called 'the father of British painting', he did not in fact have any direct followers. Sir Joshua Reynolds is the artist who in many ways appears to have a better right to the title. It is to him that belongs the credit for founding a school of painting which, although indubitably English, brought our art out of its provincial backwater and merged it into the broad European stream. In Sir Joshua, the Cinderella of British painting at last, so to speak, found her man. And it would hardly be possible to overestimate the extent of the contribution made by Italy, through his influence and that of his contemporaries, at this crucial stage in our artistic history. As one modern critic has put it: 'The plant of British painting, which had long been slowly maturing, suddenly ripened into flower about 1750 under the warmth of the Italian sun.'

It was in 1750 that Reynolds first discovered Italy when he went to Rome as a comparatively young man, and the time which he spent there was to prove as decisive for the development of British painting as the Italian tours of Inigo Jones and Lord Burlington had been for British architecture. Eighteenth-century Rome offered a vast variety of attractions for artists, but to Reynolds it was first and foremost the city where the immortal masterpieces of painting and sculpture could best be seen and studied. 'Whoever has great views', he declared, 'I would recommend to him . . . rather to live on bread and water than lose these advantages which he can never hope to enjoy a second time and which he will find only in the Vatican.' When he returned home in 1753, Reynolds soon established his reputation by painting a masterpiece of his own; and this full-length portrait of Commodore Keppel, so reminiscent of the Vatican *Apollo Belvedere* in its composition, provided the first evidence of how tremendously enriched the artist had been by his Italian experiences.

Reynolds had come back from Italy determined that it must be his mission to regenerate British art by opening the eyes of his fellow-countrymen to the supreme beauties of the works of the Italian masters. The great artists on whom he urged British painters to model their style were Raphael, Titian and, above all, Michelangelo. It may at first sight seem surprising that Michelangelo's Grand Style should have exercised such an extraordinary fascination in this country, for it has never come easily to English artists to think in the sculptural terms of Mediterranean art of which he was the consummate exponent. Part of the explanation of the paradox may be that Michelangelo appealed to our national foible for seeing art invested with literary and moral values: the English have always liked pictures to tell a story, and if it can be an edifying one, so much the better. In the time of Reynolds, moreover, his work was held to be the quintessence of 'the sublime', which was at that time revered as the supreme artistic ideal.

Already in the previous century the English sculptor Nicholas Stone had taken Michelangelo as a model; and architects had also turned to him for inspiration, as may be seen, for instance, in the New Library at Christ Church, Oxford, which is a simplified version of his Capitoline Palace in Rome. But he had been out of favour as a painter, and it was not until the impassioned advocacy of Reynolds that he was finally elevated to his unique position in the British artistic pantheon. For Reynolds, Michelangelo was the greatest artist of all time, possessing the inherent nobility of conception which he believed to be an essential attribute of the highest form of art. How much he worshipped the man whose bust he included in his own self-portrait is shown by the moving tribute which he paid him at the end of his last address to the Royal Academy, delivered shortly before he died. 'Were I now to begin the world again, I would tread in the steps of that great master: to kiss the hem of his garment. . . . I should desire', he concluded, 'that the last words which I should pronounce in this Academy, and from this place, might be the name of Michel Angelo.'

The foundation of the Royal Academy in 1768 was largely due to Reynolds. It gave British painters a new status and constituted an important milestone in Britain's artistic history. For more than two decades Reynolds used his immense authority as the Academy's first president in order to spread his gospel that the secret of great painting lay in the study and imitation of the Italian masters. The promotion of a British school of history painting was the ambition which lay particularly close to Reynolds's heart. He sought to persuade his fellow artists that they were wasting their time and talents by devoting themselves almost exclusively to the ephemeral triviality of society portraiture. He fervently believed that the highest art ought to be, like Michelangelo's, 'larger than life', as it were, and that only mythology and biblical or classical history could provide subjects sufficiently elevating to deserve the serious attention of any artist fully worthy of the name.

A certain number of history paintings were eventually to be produced in England. Often they were inspired by neo-classicism, a movement which owed a special debt of its own to Italy and Greece and which, as already mentioned, had at least a passing influence on a variety of artists including Romney and William Blake. But most of this painting was not of the kind which really met with the approval of Reynolds, and he failed to make many genuine converts to his cherished ideas.

It is not difficult to believe that Sir Joshua may have seemed rather a bore to his contemporaries when he harped on his pet theory, particularly as he did not even live up to it himself. For although he seldom scrupled to borrow from the Italian painters, he rarely attempted Michelangelo's epic subjects and the results were not particularly successful when he did. Suave and urbane, as befitted a fashionable painter in the Age of Reason, and intellectual rather than emotional, Reynolds was probably, in fact, temperamentally incapable of emulating the tragic grandeur of the master for whom he had conceived such a tremendous admiration; and it was a very different artist, William Blake, whose mysticism may have been able to find a more authentic affinity with the power and passion of the great Italian.

Reynolds was in any case not the man to despise the material rewards which his profession could offer, and it must have soon dawned on him that his fellow artists were only too likely to be right in thinking that there was not much money to be made out of history pieces. So although he continued to urge them to take the thorny road of history painting, he was usually prudent enough to keep to the primrose path of portraiture himself.

Ever since the Reformation had put an end to the demand for religious pictures, portraits had been practically the only kind of paintings which the English wanted. Even in Reynolds's day it was still much the same. The wealthy aristocracy, who were virtually the only patrons of the arts, considered it a highly desirable status-symbol to have their portraits done by some fashionable painter. But they were, on the other hand, hardly ever prepared to give an English artist a commission for any other kind of work.

So even Reynolds, supremely influential though he might be, found himself obliged to come to terms with the English passion for portraiture. But although he failed to dethrone the portrait from its dominant position in the British artistic tradition, he was at least successful in creating a synthesis between portraiture and the epic style of history painting, teaching his contemporaries how portraits could be painted with a noble dignity and elegance deriving their inspiration from Van Dyck and the Italian High Renaissance, which had taught him richness of colour and nobility of design. The famous Grand Manner of his portraiture can be seen at its most relentlessly classical in his *Lady Sarah Bunbury sacrificing to the Graces*; whilst the pose in *Mrs Siddons as the Tragic Muse* was actually based on the figure of Isaiah on the Sistine ceiling. Portraits like that of Lady Hertford are invested with a classical timelessness: drawing, once again, the general out of the particular, he sees her as a beauty, not merely of her day, but of all time.

It may have been largely thanks to the influence of Reynolds, at a period when the general taste was as Italianized as his own, that by the time of his death in 1792, British portraiture could stand comparison with any contemporary school in Europe. During his own generation and the next, there emerged a series of portrait painters of the charm and distinction of Romney, Raeburn, Gainsborough and Lawrence. Each of them owed something to the Italian manner which he so forcefully advocated, and all except Gainsborough had followed his example by going to the fountainhead and studying in Italy itself.

When British art reached maturity in the fullness of time, painters inevitably tended to become more independent of foreign inspiration; and the Italian Renaissance naturally had less to teach them once the classical age of British painting, over which Reynolds had so long presided, gave way to the Romantic period. Before leaving the subject of Italy's influence on British portrait painting, however, it remains to mention a different type of portraiture which originated in that country but was subsequently developed in our own by artists like Hogarth, Rowlandson and Gillray.

The 'caricatura' seems to have been first invented at the end of the sixteenth century by the Roman painter, Annibale Carracci. Caricature portraits became popular with English visitors on the Grand Tour: just as the modern tourist likes to bring back photographs of his fellow-travellers, so the eighteenth-century tourist would often commission some artist in Rome or Florence to do a 'caricatura' sketch of his companions which he could take home with him as a memento. But after these relatively modest beginnings, the English quickly discovered that the caricature could offer moral, social and humorous possibilities which were particularly attractive to their taste. Soon, too, the satirical cartoon became a powerful weapon in British politics.

But the British cannot claim ever to have produced a Titian or Velasquez. This may have been partly perhaps because British art developed so late. By the time that it finally matured in the middle of the eighteenth century, landscape painting, previously serving as little more than the incidental background of the picture and regarded as only a subsidiary form of European art, was acquiring an enhanced status. And it is in landscape, even more than in portraiture, that the English school has made its most distinctive contribution to the western artistic heritage.

This is a branch of art which has proved particularly congenial to the native temperament. As a nation the English are romantics with an instinctive love of nature; and from the point of view of the painter himself, the soft, misty light typical of this northern climate has an enchantment of its own. But although landscape painting eventually came to be regarded as a very characteristically English medium of artistic expression, in its beginnings it was affected by Mediterranean influences no less strongly than English portraiture had been. The other most significant early influence was the Dutch. But initially at least, Italian idealism was thought to be a nobler source of inspiration than the humbler realism of the Dutch painters.

Already at the opening of the eighteenth century, a demand was developing in England for landscape, or at any rate for topographical painting. The Georgian patricians soon began to want paintings of the parks and houses in which they took such pride, almost as much as they wanted pictures of themselves; and if they had gone on the Grand Tour, they were also often anxious to have some pictorial record of what they had seen on their travels. At the same time, they needed big canvases to furnish the vast rooms of the new mansions they were building, and large landscape pictures in the Italian manner were considered to be eminently suitable for such a purpose.

The remarkable success which Canaletto achieved in this country is not difficult to understand, therefore. Here was a topographical artist admirably equipped to satisfy all these requirements. The elegance of his manner of depicting fine architecture delighted a generation which set so much store by splendid buildings. There could be few more appropriate ornaments for any gentleman's residence than his handsome pictures of Italy or of the English scene (to which he knew how to give the fashionable Italian flavour). So his works were eagerly sought after by the connoisseurs. A number of them found their way into the collection of George III, and many of his most important paintings have remained in England to this day.

Canaletto had acquired a clientèle of patrons amongst the English aristocrats visiting Venice on the Grand Tour. It was thanks to their encouragement that he came over to England in 1746. The views which he painted of London in the early months after his arrival, whilst the bright southern light was still fresh in his memory, invested the Thames with a radiant luminosity reminiscent of the Grand Canal in Canaletto's own city.

Pictures of such allure naturally found many imitators here. But although Canaletto was the first Italian painter of genuine distinction ever to work in this country for any considerable length of time, his influence on the development of British art and taste could not in the long run compare with that of the artists who had painted in Rome during the previous century. It is not Canaletto, or even the Poussins or Salvator Rosa, but Claude Lorraine who is the main strand running through the formative years in the history of British landscape painting.

Claude Gelée had been born in Lorraine in 1600 but he spent most of his working life in Rome. Classical scenes set in Roman ruins were his favourite subjects, and he approached them with an intense feeling for the picturesque which often anticipates Romanticism. His compositions may not have attained quite the same nobility as those of Nicolas Poussin but, being less intellectual, they provided a more acceptable model for English artists when they were first striving to learn how to organize the landscape into a pictorial shape. The earliest English landscape painters largely depended, moreover, on commissions from noblemen requiring picturesque views of their parks and properties; and it would be difficult to imagine an artist better able to inspire a flattering picture of such subjects than Claude, who seems to have imagined the whole of nature as if laid out for man's delight in a kind of park-like Garden of Eden.

Eighteenth-century Englishmen discovered in Claude's paintings an ideal of natural beauty which fascinated them to the point of obsession. He appealed to both the romantic and the classical in their temperament. His dreams became their dreams. For the classical tastes of the Augustan age, the cool simplicity of his 'Virgilian' pastorals seemed the acme of perfection. Poets as well as painters sought inspiration in his idyllic visions, and landscape designers took his gentle poetry as their model. Even Reynolds, who was not usually inclined to rate landscape painters very high, made an exception in favour of this artist who, he said, 'conducts us to the tranquillity of Arcadian scenes and fairy-land', and he included several of Claude's works in his own collection.

It was to Richard Wilson, who had an instinctive affinity with Claude, that it fell to play a role in the development of British landscape painting comparable with that of Reynolds in British portraiture. Like Reynolds, Wilson first discovered Italy in the year 1750 and, like Reynolds again, he became steeped in the Mediterranean tradition as a result of his stay there. After spending a period in Venice, he proceeded to study in Rome, and it was there that he fell under the spell of the enchanted landscape of the Campagna, just as Claude had done a century before him.

The Roman countryside has exercised a perennial fascination over artists. Laurence Binyon has described the Campagna, 'with its wide plain bordered by noble hills, its lakes lying in wooded hollows, its majestic remains of Roman monuments, its broken aqueducts and tombs; a serene and ordered landscape, perfumed with associations, breathing of a great past'. In the days of Claude, and even in Wilson's own, the scene must have been more numinous still. This was the pastoral landscape with which Wilson fell in love. It gave him a profoundly moving vision of an ideal beauty – a revelation that was hardly less unforgettable for him than Michelangelo's Sistine Chapel had been for Reynolds; and it is there that lies a key to the painting of both these artists.

Italy brought Wilson a new conception of natural beauty which persuaded him to abandon portraiture and devote himself to landscape. That country never ceased to haunt his imagination, continuing to inspire his work long after he had returned to England. Many of his later pictures were Italian landscapes painted from memory or from sketches which he had brought back from Rome. Even when he took his subjects from nearer home, he usually treated them with the same classical serenity, and he sometimes seems to have seen his native Wales as if it were bathed in the clear light of a Mediterranean summer.

Richard Wilson was influenced not only by the Roman landscape itself, but also by the artists who had painted it with such exquisite lyricism a century before, and who were now able to provide him with an element of orderliness and organization with which to temper his own romanticism. His painting shares the dreamlike quality of Claude, and it was from the latter that he learnt the secret of giving his pictures a centre of radiant luminosity. But this does not mean that Wilson merely contented himself with producing set-pieces in the Claudian manner. He had a genuine feeling for the beauty of nature which he expressed in a quiet poetry of his own, far removed from any Latin grandiloquence. In the words of John Ruskin, it was with Wilson that there began in England 'sincere landscape art founded on the meditative love of nature'.

Whilst the kind of public recognition achieved by Reynolds never came Wilson's way, many lesser painters followed in his footsteps although, lacking his originality, they were usually inclined to adhere more closely to the conventional classical tradition. One of the most gifted of them was J. R. Cozens, the author of a number of enchanting watercolours of Italy. Another was Francis Towne. A more individual artist was Joseph Wright, who was lucky enough to witness an eruption of Vesuvius, a phenomenon which stimulated his passionate interest in the effects of light and gave him the theme for a remarkable series of romantic studies. There was also the Victorian artist Samuel Palmer, the last in the long sequence of painters of the 'Virgilian' landscape, before scientific materialism made such visions of the ideal past seem absurdly irrelevant.

All these painters lived for a time in Italy, just as Wilson and Reynolds had done before them. Many others did the same, often getting work there from some young patron on his Grand Tour. Whilst romantics like Bonington and Turner were usually drawn most of all to Venice, the majority of these painters congregated in Rome, where the narrow streets round the Piazza di Spagna became so overrun with English artists that they were called the 'Ghetto degl'Inglesi'. Thomas Hollis had voiced the accepted opinion when he pronounced: 'Undoubtedly, Italian, and especially Roman air, if properly imbibed, is of all others the most pure and nourishing to the artist.' Some, in fact, found the draught so intoxicating that they never managed to tear themselves away at all: their doyen was Gavin Hamilton, who settled permanently in Rome to paint a series of huge history pieces.

There were many good reasons to tempt any young English painter to Rome. It was then the great meeting-place for European artists, whose stimulus and emulation might encourage him to shed his insularity. Under better teachers than at home, he had unrivalled opportunities of studying the finest masterpieces of Renaissance art in the galleries. The ruins and churches of the city itself, like the beauty of the surrounding countryside, offered an inexhaustible supply of picturesque subjects for his painting. All this went to shape the artist's taste and style. He would have had to be insensitive indeed to resist the manifold attractions of this supremely evocative city; and if he happened to be a landscape painter, he could hardly fail to fall under the spell of its splendid setting.

More remarkable, perhaps, is the way that even English painters who never managed to get to Italy at all felt the magic of a landscape which they could only know at second hand, from prints and paintings, and were equally eager to conform to the fashionable Italian convention. An artist of such strong individual genius as Gainsborough might have been expected to provide the exception to prove the rule. He too, however, although he never set foot in Italy, seems to have allowed the prevailing Italianate prejudices to inhibit him from giving a completely free rein to the expression of his natural feeling for the English landscape. Whilst he loved the quiet English countryside, he insisted on arranging it in picturesque landscape 'compositions' in his sketches. And in one of his letters he significantly complains that nowhere in England had he ever found a subject 'equal to the poorest imitations of Gaspar or Claude'. For Gainsborough and his contemporaries it was in fact almost impossible to believe that any scenery outside Italy could really be worth painting, or that the straightforward imitation of nature could ever be as high a form of art as were imaginative compositions in the Italian manner; and if the latter could be infused with 'picturesque' literary associations, whether historical or mythological, then so much the better.

Although tastes changed when the Romantic tide started to gather force later in the century, the sober classicism of Poussin and Claude still seems to have hardly begun to pall. But for those who might now find these Roman artists a little tame, there was yet another seventeenth-century Italian painter, Salvator Rosa, with a very different style which was admirably suited to satisfy the new craze for 'the Picturesque'. This Neapolitan romantic, whose sense of drama was deliberately horrific, filled his pictures with crags and rocks, gibbets and bandits. His theatrical rhetoric may seem a trifle preposterous to the modern taste. At that time, however, it undoubtedly helped to give a fresh dimension to the growing English appreciation of nature, so that wild and mountainous scenery now became almost more popular than the gentle Arcadian landscape associated with Claude. Even Gainsborough himself sometimes allowed himself to attempt to imitate Salvator's 'terrible sublimity'.

It was only after gradually adapting Italian principles to the English environment that artists at last grew to understand that it was better simply to paint the real scenery of their own country rather than imaginary visions in the Italian manner. It had taken them an unconscionable time. Horace Walpole summed it up in his *Anecdotes of Painting*: 'In a country so profusely beautiful with the amenities of nature, it is extraordinary that we have produced so few good painters of landscapes. As our poets warm their imaginations with sunny hills, or sigh after grottoes and cooling breezes, our painters draw rocks and precipices and castellated mountains, because Virgil gasped for breath at Naples, and Salvator wandered amidst Alps and Apennines.'

Naturalism did not finally win the day until Wordsworth and the other Romantic poets had invested the love of the simple beauty of nature with an almost religious significance. The English were then at length prepared to appreciate nature for its own sake and look at it with their own eyes, instead of through the eyes of the painters of Italy – or through what was called a 'Claude glass', the tinted device so frequently used by the eighteenth-century gentleman in order to enable him to see the view in an appropriately soft and mellow glow. At long last, the Italian formula no longer seemed to people to be such an indispensable recipe for the painting of their own landscape.

But there is abundant evidence in English art and literature well on into the nineteenth century, to show that the hallowed traditions did not entirely lose their hold even then. Constable himself, who said that he never saw an ugly thing in his life, and who is generally regarded as the first English painter to discover the art of unquestioning naturalism, always retained his faithful admiration for the 'ideal' Italian landscape. As Kenneth Clark has remarked, his deep under-standing of the principles of European landscape painting was 'one of the reasons why Constable was able to present such a quantity of normal observation without the painful banality of later realists'.

In spite of his ardent belief in the virtues of direct observation, Constable would frequently leave his own painting aside in order to copy a Poussin or a Claude. He had a particular devotion to the latter, calling him 'the most perfect landscape painter the world ever saw . . . something to drink at again and again'. And he once wrote to his wife: 'I do not wonder at your being jealous of Claude. If anything could come between our love, it is him.'

In the case of the most revolutionary of all the English landscape painters, J. M. W. Turner, Italian influences were to play an even more important and complex role, however. If Turner had never gone to Italy, greatness might have eluded him, and he would have perhaps remained the precociously successful but rather pedestrian painter of his earlier period when he was generally content merely to produce pastiches of the landscapes of Claude. Although these pictures enjoyed an enormous popularity in England at the time, they nowadays seem a somewhat uneasy compromise between classical restraint and Turner's natural romanticism. He admired Titian and had a higher regard for Poussin than any other British artist of his day. But being essentially a romantic in his approach to nature, he was well aware that in reality he had most in common with Claude and the style which Wilson had evolved from him. For many years, indeed, Turner's fondest ambition was to emulate the painter whose *Embarkation of the Queen of Sheba* he sought to rival with his own *Dido building Carthage*, which he bequeathed to the National Gallery on the condition that the two pictures should always be hung side by side.

When he reached greater maturity, however, Turner, whilst never losing his love for his mentor Claude, could no longer be fully satisfied with the rather facile kind of picturesque, Italianate painting which had brought him such popular acclaim. He began to feel the need for a more individual form of expression. Like many other artists in the century which was to see the birth of the Impressionist movement, Turner became increasingly engrossed with problems of the effects of light. But until he first saw Italy in middle age, he does not seem to have trusted his intensely personal vision sufficiently to push his experiments very far towards their logical conclusion.

Sir Thomas Lawrence, the portrait painter who became the president of the Royal Academy, had written from Rome in 1819 that Italy would provide Turner with exactly what he needed for the development of his genius. This was prescient advice. Turner's Italian experiences, by encouraging him to give full play to his exceptional sense of colour, were destined to prove a turning-point in his artistic development no less decisive than their own had been for Reynolds and Richard Wilson before him.

Turner followed the fashion by going first of all to Rome, where he found subjects for a number of exquisite sketches. But he was now beginning to discard the classicism which he had derived from Poussin and Claude, so that it was in the romantic setting of Venice that he instinctively felt more in his element. He painted Venice as though it had been a phantom city, suspended between sky and water; and the time that he spent there, brief though it in fact was, had a profound influence on the development of his later style.

As with Van Gogh, another northern artist who became possessed with a similar passion for brilliant colour, it is impossible to imagine that the genius of Turner would have matured in the extraordinary way it did if it had not been for the revelation of the Mediterranean. There he discovered a world of dazzling brightness surpassing his wildest dreams. The weeks which he spent in Venice finally liberated his emotions. By opening his eyes to intoxicating possibilities of colour in which he had hardly dared believe before he saw the South, they gave him confidence to create his apocalyptic rhapsodies in praise of light.

It is easy to understand that many of Turner's Victorian contemporaries should have been mystified and shocked when they were confronted with pictures like his filmy, shimmering visions of *Norham Castle*, which were so utterly different from the decorous sobriety of the familiar pseudo-classical landscapes they had hitherto been accustomed to expect from him. John Constable said that Turner seemed to have painted them with 'tinted steam'. But whatever their defects of drawing and composition, their violent yet very delicate colour, anticipating Monet and the French Impressionists, gives these paintings an almost magical quality, and it is mainly on them that his fame rests for us today. Seeking as he did the ultimate intensity of luminosity, yellow held a special fascination for him; and if the story is true that Turner's dying words were 'The Sun is God', his imagination must surely have been harking back at the end to the radiance which the Mediterranean had first revealed to him.

The spectacular release of Turner's sense of colour values, which enabled him to attain what John Ruskin called his 'unique luxury of colour', was to be the last great debt British painting would owe to Italian influences (although it may not be entirely without significance that it was his expert knowledge of the Italian Old Masters that later helped the critic Roger Fry to become the first champion of Post-Impressionist art in England). The great Ruskin himself took the lead in discrediting the painters who had traditionally inspired us. As an art critic his influence was at that time unsurpassed, and his scathing attacks on the Poussins, 'filmy, futile Claude', and Salvator Rosa, 'the dissipated jester', played a large part in bringing to a close this long and illustrious chapter in the history of British art.

The Victorian period can scarcely be described as a conspicuously artistic age. Turner's freedom of handling paint and colour was strong meat for the popular taste which preferred meticulous realism. Other English painters were too timid to imitate him, and when a new style emerged shortly before he died, it preferred to ignore his revolutionary discoveries. Being obsessed with realism, the Pre-Raphaelites turned their back on naturalism. Although this movement took a good deal from Italy besides its name, it was essentially an example of the English predilection for decorative illustration, as opposed to plastic form. Its high sentiment had, in reality, little in common with the true spirit of Mediterranean art.

The Pre-Raphaelite Brotherhood had been founded in 1848 by a small group of British artists who rebelled against the prevailing fashion of attempting feeble imitations of the Old Masters, tracing this back to the influence of Sir Joshua Reynolds whom they dubbed 'Sir Sloshua'. The Pre-Raphaelites dreamed of a purer art inspired by more primitive painters and by nature itself. Despite their name, they were almost as ignorant of Raphael's precursors as were the great majority of other English people at that time. They placed some of the later Renaissance painters very high, however. The list of 'Immortals' compiled by Hunt and Rossetti included not only Titian and Tintoretto, but even Raphael himself, for the movement was not hostile to Raphael as it believed he really was, but only to what academic art had made of him.

But the Pre-Raphaelites themselves were guilty of misinterpreting the great Italians in their own earnest, well-intentioned fashion, and despite their lofty aspirations, their art soon deteriorated into a sentimental and nostalgic archaism. The Pre-Raphaelite attempt to redeem Victorian art had, in fact, been misconceived, and British painting was now returning to the provincialism from which a better understanding of Italian artistic principles had rescued it a century before. But there is at least one by-product of the Pre-Raphaelite movement which may have stood the test of time more successfully than the paintings themselves. For it was the versatile craftsmanship of William Morris and the splendid type, deriving from the Italian Renaissance, which he adopted for his book production, that helped to make English printing a model of its kind.

By the time the Pre-Raphaelite Brotherhood dissolved shortly after the middle of the century, the great revolution in French painting had begun, and Paris was soon to take the place so long held by Rome as the Mecca for Europe's artists. Eventually, after an unhappy interval when this country produced, in the words of Hippolyte Taine, pictures 'unbelievably disagreeable to look at', English painting came once again to play a role within the main stream of the European tradition. But by then the dominant influences had long ceased to be Italian.

What kind of balance-sheet can be drawn up of Italy's contribution to British painting during the most famous period in its history? This Anglo-Italian relationship was bound to be a chequered one, and it would be idle to pretend that it proved an unmixed blessing. There is a great gulf fixed between the classical temperament of the Italians and our own natural romanticism, and it is no surprise to find that much of what was most characteristic of British painting in fact owed little or nothing to Italy. English taste has usually, for instance, particularly delighted in literary and moral overtones such as are to be found in the pictures of Hogarth or the Pre-Raphaelites, whereas the painting of plastic form and of the nude has never been central to our artistic tradition in the way that it has been to the Italian.

It is seldom easy for an English artist to treat his subject with the plastic precision which the hard clarity of Mediterranean light requires. His instinctive preference is for the poetry and half-tones of impression, and for line, the sinuous 'Gothic' line, rather than for form. Apart from a few rare exceptions, as notably in the case of Turner, there were not many English painters who were entirely successful in evolving a satisfactory formula for rendering the brilliant luminosity of the South. Some of them might even prefer to by-pass the difficulties altogether, as in Edward Lear's modest topographical understatements, with their emphasis on sensitive design with a bare minimum of colour.

By no means all the young English artists who flocked to Rome could be expected to have either the temperament or the experience required to solve the unfamiliar problems that they found facing them there. The Italian training which they received must often have run against the natural grain of their talent: there was a risk that their artistic development would be diverted from its normal bent, and that they might be encouraged to take refuge in a sterile academism. Those of them who were capable of rising to the challenge were much richer for it. Sometimes, however, the artists who stayed at home in England seem to have been better able to benefit from the classical tradition than were those who directly exposed themselves to the alien and disturbing world of the Mediterranean.

And even if it is hard to believe that any other country could have so well provided what British painting most needed during its formative period, it could still be objected that British artists were inclined to take more from Italy than was really good for them. Although the discipline of the classical ideal may have been almost indispensable to them at the start, it is arguable that they allowed themselves to be obsessed for too long by the Grand Style, or by Claude and the other painters of the Mediterranean landscape. There must have come a time when the weight of the Italian conventions would have seemed a little overpowering. It may have delayed the growth of a genuine national style, which could only reach full maturity when British painters had acquired sufficient self-confidence to cast off their Italian leading-strings.

But even if all this were to be conceded, it would still be fair to say that in painting the British were no less beholden to Italy than they were in most of the other arts. As has been seen, the art of portraiture did not mature in England until Reynolds had inculcated the style of the Renaissance masters. It was largely thanks to Italy, too, that we first learned to appreciate nature and landscape, and British artists might never have succeeded in taking such a distinguished place amongst the landscape painters of Europe if they had not first felt the inspiration of Italian painters and of Italian skies.

It would similarly be difficult to dispute that it was primarily owing to its contact with the Mediterranean traditions that British eighteenth-century art acquired the sophistication and refinement which gave it its characteristic blend of dignity, elegance and harmony. And even after our native painters had become more independent of their Italian tutelage and learnt to stand on their own feet, the best of them generally retained sufficient understanding of classical principles to save them from the whimsical prettiness which is so liable to be the besetting sin of British art. All said and done therefore, it can scarcely be denied that British painting would have been not only a very different, but also almost certainly an infinitely poorer thing if Italian influences had not done so much to mould it.

CHAPTER 6

ART INTO LANDSCAPE

Not so very long ago it might have seemed an absurd paradox, but nowadays it has become almost a truism to say that nature, or at least the cultivated man's conception of nature, will often copy art. We are well aware that great art opens our eyes to natural beauty. We can hardly help seeing the landscape through the eyes of the poets and painters whose imagination has idealized it for us, so that our view of nature tends to be a reflection of their own.

Certainly, our eighteenth-century ancestors were particularly prone to see nature in terms of the preconceived ideas which they had derived from poetry and philosophy and, above all, from painting. The picturesque fantasies of Claude and the other painters of the Mediterranean landscape provided the most attractive vision of natural beauty which they believed to be possible. As this was their ideal of ultimate perfection, they instinctively turned to it for inspiration when creating the splendid gardens with which they civilized the face of England.

The Duke of Wellington once remarked that the English park was the greatest contribution made by the British to the arts; and few people would disagree that it was at any rate the supreme artistic achievement of the English amateur. What may be less generally recognized, however, is the extent of the debt which this owes to

Italian influences. The gardening of landscape gave us our countryside. Much of what now seems to us not only most beautiful but also most typically English in our essentially man-made landscape, was in reality deliberately fashioned in the likeness of the poetic and pictorial images of Italy which exercised such an irresistible fascination over the imagination of the age. It would scarcely be an exaggeration to say, therefore, that in eighteenth-century England, nature was often almost literally transformed into a copy of art.

By the eighteenth century, it had become the ambition of English landowners, who were then at the heyday of their prosperity and power, not only to possess as magnificent a house as possible, but also to use its surroundings in such a way as to give it an appropriate and equally splendid setting. This enthusiastic interest in the pictorial possibilities of the landscape was something relatively new. In earlier times wild nature had been regarded with awe and apprehension, and centuries were to elapse before the western Europeans developed a genuine appreciation of scenery. Even a man as sophisticated as John Evelyn, writing as late as the middle of the seventeenth century, could only find the lovely forest of Fontainebleau 'horrid and solitary' and full of 'hideous rocks'.

So long as this primitive mistrust of untamed nature persisted, a garden had to be protected and enclosed: it was an oasis of civilization sheltered from a dangerous and hostile outside world. Thus in the days of the Tudors, medieval walled gardens still remained the general rule, although some sixteenth-century English travellers brought back a taste for the formal Renaissance garden, and famous gardens in the Italian style were laid out by Robert Cecil at Hatfield House and by John Danvers in Chelsea.

It was not until after the Restoration that any major change took place. The scene then became dominated by Le Nôtre, the great French architect who perfected the Baroque conception of the 'garden of reason', with an elaborate geometrical symmetry unified by a grand design. His pupils worked at St James's Park and Hampton Court, and every landed gentleman dreamt of possessing a miniature Versailles of his own. Equally formal in their different way were the Dutch gardens introduced in William III's time, which were remarkable for their elaborate topiary work, an art originally invented in Imperial Rome.

During the reign of George I, however, both the smooth French parterres and the Dutch gardens were swept away, and the English garden passed from the studied formality of a kind of open-air drawing room to an informal naturalism which was equally contrived. The traditional concept of the garden as an extension of the architecture of the house became outmoded. Taste now, on the contrary, demanded a 'natural' garden, whose elegant irregularity should make an agreeably romantic contrast to the classical formality of the new style of Palladian house, whilst at the same time blending effortlessly with the surrounding landscape. So nature at last came into fashion and the lovely poetry of 'natural' gardening began.

This was not, of course, simply a revolution in taste. Other, more mundane factors were involved as well. The change from stag to fox hunting required a different style of park; and there was also a powerful economic incentive for this large-scale replanting of the countryside at a time when wood for shipbuilding was in short supply. Timber had, in fact, by this time become a better investment than corn or wool.

The Georgian patricians who rearranged the face of England in such noble style must, however, be allowed credit for more elevated motives too. This was the great Age of Taste. A correct taste in landscape was deemed an eminently desirable social accomplishment; and it was generally accepted that a gentleman's country place ought to be made a thing of beauty, and not regarded merely as a source of profit. Every landowner wanted not only his house but his whole property to be more handsome and up-to-date than his neighbour's, and money would not be stinted on its embellishment.

If this was largely ostentation, at least it was ostentation which produced results of the most admirable kind. Moreover, it would be fair to say that, grossly materialistic though they might be in other ways, surprisingly often these eighteenth-century tycoons seem to have possessed a genuine feeling for higher things. In many cases their sensibility to artistic and natural beauty would have been first awakened by their youthful travels on the Grand Tour. But others too, although they might never have seen Italy, developed a similar passion for the Italian landscape which was familiar to them from poetry and painting.

A late eighteenth-century critic said that the admiration for Italian scenery which led the English to superimpose it on their own landscape stemmed partly from the classical education which prejudiced them in favour of everything connected with antiquity, but most of all from the paintings of this scenery which had given them their 'first impressions of the Beauty of Nature'. At the start, however, when Italy and its painters were still not widely known in England, it was only the English poets who appear to have adopted a pictorial approach to the landscape. Landscape was their province, and already in the previous century there had been evidence that the painted landscapes of Rubens, Titian and Claude were influencing their imagination.

The reaction against the artificiality of French and Dutch gardens thus began as a literary and philosophical revolt. The English writers derived their initial ideas of a simpler and more natural garden from their favourite classical authors. It was from Latin poetry that they discovered that the ancient Romans, whom they were always so eager to take as their model, had often preferred to leave their villas surrounded with 'the amiable simplicity of unadorned nature'. At the beginning of the century, the philosopher Lord Shaftesbury acclaimed wild nature as more magnificent than 'the formal mockery of princely gardens'. Similar sentiments were soon to be expressed by writers like Addison and Pope, and the latter put the new theories into practice when he laid out his own little garden at Twickenham in 1719. The first landscape-gardens do not seem to have been primarily visual: rather they were poetic compositions seeking to carry the imagination back to the Arcadian world of Virgil and Theocritus.

But Pope himself declared that 'all gardening is landscape-painting', and painting, after helping to inspire the poets, soon replaced literature as the chief source of inspiration for the English landscape-gardeners. An expression which became increasingly popular as the century wore on, and the English grew more alive to the aesthetic possibilities of scenery, was 'picturesque'. The word was derived from the Italian 'pittoresco' ('after the manner of painters'). In those days it had, however, a rather different meaning from the one it has today. The adjective was applied to the kind of landscape so happily arranged that it looked as if it had come out of a painting; and the more a landscape could be 'improved' so as to resemble a picture, the more it was considered to be deserving of admiration.

With the spread of the fashion for the picturesque, Dutch and Flemish pictures were sometimes taken as models. But their realism never made such a wide appeal to the English as the 'grand' scenery associated with Claude and Nicolas Poussin, or the 'savage' scenery of Salvator Rosa, and it was these painters of the Italian landscape who were generally held to be the best guides of how nature should be looked at and be made to look. Salvator was thought to be especially 'picturesque', as may be gathered from the young Horace Walpole's celebrated comment on the Alps, 'precipices, mountains, torrents, wolves, rumblings – Salvator Rosa. . . .' The 'horrible majesty' of his moors and mountains could excite a not unpleasant 'frisson' in eighteenth-century breasts, and would eventually help the English to develop an appreciation of wild scenery:

> Horrors like these at first alarm,
> But soon with savage grandeur charm,
> And raise to noblest thoughts the mind . . .
> A pleasing, tho' an awful sight.

For an age so passionately interested in the classical, however, the noble Roman compositions of 'soft Claude' possessed an even greater fascination than the Neapolitan melodrama of 'dashing, daring Salvator'. Claude's blend of classicism and romanticism chimed perfectly with English tastes, and no other painter knew how to invest antiquity with such nostalgic glamour. Landscape-gardeners might sometimes borrow 'picturesque effects' from Salvator (like William Kent who went so far as to plant dead trees in Kensington Gardens). But when they sought to recapture a vision of the ideal past, it was Claude's tranquil beauty that could best inspire them.

The English love of these painters helped to awaken their sensitivity to natural beauty, as seems to have been realized by the critic who wrote at the end of the eighteenth century that if the Greek poets had had so little to say about picturesque scenery, it must have been because there were no painters, 'no Claudes', to open their eyes to it.

The appreciation of landscape comes so naturally to the present-day Englishman that it is easy to assume that it has always been one of our national characteristics. Even as late, however, as the middle of the century, in the urbane Augustan Age, although country gentlemen had by then long been making their gardens into illusions of tamed nature, wild nature was still considered distressingly uncouth compared with the ideal landscape in Italian painting. It was only gradually that the taste for scenery developed, as a result of seeing it, as it were, through the eyes of the Italian artists and of the landscape-gardeners who imitated them. The process was not really complete until Wordsworth and other Romantic poets, fired by Rousseau's new cult of Nature, and spurning the artificialities of the picturesque, preached the virtues of bucolic simplicity, unimproved and unadorned.

Thus, it is in fact scarcely two centuries ago that the English, after their taste had first been educated by Italian painting, developed into a nation of nature poets and landscape painters, and the love of nature and scenery came to take an important place in their way of life. This coincided with the time when far more people found themselves obliged to live in large cities than ever had before. But by then even town-dwellers were trying to retain at least an illusion of the country-side: Buckingham Palace itself was not built as a town palace but as an early nineteenth-century country house, whilst the London squares, which originally had the formality of Italian piazzas, were later designed to give an impression of rustic informality – 'rus in urbe'.

For much of the eighteenth century, however, the educated Englishman still found it almost impossible to appreciate scenery except in terms of Italian painting. One of the principal pleasures of travelling was to discover picturesque Italian effects in the English landscape. A popular guide to the Lake District published in 1778 shows the extraordinary lengths to which this craze was pushed. The author conducts the tourist 'from the delicate touches of Claude, verified on Coniston-lake, to the noble scenes of Poussin exhibited on Windermere-water, and from there to the stupendous romantic ideas of Salvator Rosa, realized in the lake of Derwent'. The mania for the Picturesque affected literature as well. The word frequently occurs in the novels of Jane Austen, for instance (and the first mention of a 'walk' in English fiction was that taken by Elizabeth Bennett in *Pride and Prejudice*); and by her day, a failure to appreciate nature was evidently felt to denote a lack of sensibility. As has already been seen, even architecture was not immune to the fashion, and one of John Nash's less successful inventions was a 'picturesque' type of house deliberately modelled on the buildings in Claude's pictures.

But it was above all in their gardens that the English sought to translate the poetic visions of Italy's artists into reality. The eighteenth-century gentleman took a passionate interest in landscape-gardening. His park was the fulfilment of his dreams and he had a romantic longing to give his pastoral landscape the semblance of some lost paradise. He saw it as a painting, a vision of Italy such as Claude or Gaspard Poussin might have imagined, thus evoking an ideal picture as well as an ideal past.

No landscape-gardener could satisfy this new craving for the picturesque better than Lord Burlington's protégé William Kent, the protean artist who started as a painter and finally became 'dictator of design in everything'. Even earlier fashionable practitioners of the less formal style were Switzer and Charles Bridgeman. The latter began remodelling the great gardens at Stowe which were soon to be regarded as the finest expression of the concept of Ideal Nature. He also anticipated Kent in experimenting with the serpentine (acclaimed by Hogarth as 'the Line of Beauty'), and he was probably responsible for the design of the Serpentine in Hyde Park. Bridgeman's most fruitful contribution to the new gardening, however, may have been to perfect the ha-ha, an ingenious device to keep out animals so that the garden could be left open to the countryside. Horace Walpole, himself a keen gardener, acknowledged this technical invention to be 'a capital stroke leading to all that has followed'. But it was Kent whom Walpole called 'the father of modern gardening', the supreme landscape-architect 'who leaped the fence and saw that all nature was a garden'.

The years which he spent studying painting in Rome in the second decade of the eighteenth century had given Kent the opportunity to discover the Italian artists and the Virgilian landscape which inspired them. In the great gardens he designed after his return from Italy he sought to recreate the world of fantasy of these ideal Italian landscapes. Walpole describes one of Kent's gardens as recalling 'such exact pictures of Claude Lorrain that it is difficult to conceive that he did not paint them from this very spot'. At Stowe, Kent translated Claude's idyllic vision of the Campagna into English 'Elysian Fields', giving this name, itself so evocative of Claude, to part of the grounds. Of his masterpiece at Rousham, Walpole declared, 'the whole is as elegant and antique as if the Emperor Julian had selected the most pleasing solitude about Daphne'. Whilst another of his creations, the garden at Holkham which was Kent's own favourite, moved a poet to write that 'learned Poussin gives each grace to flow, and bright Lorrain's ethereal colours glow'.

Once this English Claude Lorraine had shown to what noble effect the landscape could be 'improved' so as to resemble the Ideal Nature of the Italian painters, the passion for 'improvement' soon swept everything before it, with noblemen like Burlington, Leicester, Pelham, Bathurst and Temple in the van of the new fashion. Perhaps it is at Stourhead Park in Wiltshire that is to be found the most exquisite of all these evocations of the Claudian Arcadia. But there are many others. For all over the shires, landscape-architects set to work laying out parks of splendid trees, with artificial hills and valleys, lakes and winding streams. 'Every Man now', says a journal of 1739, 'be his fortune what it will, is *doing something at his Place*, as the Phrase is. . . . A *Serpentine River*, and a *Wood* are become absolute Necessaries of Life.'

Yet another 'Necessary of Life' was a ruin. No eighteenth-century gentleman's park was complete without one. It could be classical or Gothic, but a Greek or a Roman temple was considered a particularly desirable ornament. Since genuine ancient ruins were not easy to

come by, most people had to make do with shams. Sir William
Chambers, for example, constructed a fake Roman ruin in Kew
Gardens. Often, however, they contained genuine antique material,
like the Roman stones from Leptis Magna set up by George IV at
Virginia Water, or the statues from Hadrian's villa in the grounds of
Chiswick House. Sometimes the complete remains of an ancient
building would be transported from Italy, as when Robert Adam
brought over the Temple of Minerva Medica to put in the park at
Kedleston.

Such 'becoming objects' were not mere whimsical eccentricities.
Sir Joshua Reynolds had given his authority to the importance of
including a ruin in the Ideal Landscape, and Claude had often put ruins
in his own works. When once it had become accepted that a garden
must be laid out so as to look like a picture, a ruin might become as
necessary for its design as it was in the composition of a painting.
Nothing could be so agreeably picturesque or more suitably provide
what the Earl of Chatham called 'a considerable object to terminate
the vista'. This is not the whole explanation of the craze, however.
The extraordinary fascination of ruins for eighteenth-century taste was
partly antiquarian, for antiquities recalling the classical past were very
much in fashion, but above all it was romantic. Their associations
could provoke a wide variety of edifying emotions, and it was felt that
sublime pleasure might be derived from visiting a garden where an
Arcadian landscape had been nostalgically embellished with such
evocative reminders of the frailty of human achievement.

After William Kent the most famous name in landscape-gardening
is Lancelot Brown, whom a poet of the time described as 'a great
painter' who turned into reality,

> What'er Lorraine light-touched with softening hue,
> Or savage Rosa dash'd, or learned Poussin drew.

Thanks to his exceptional gift for assessing what he called the
'capabilities' of grounds (by which he meant the possibilities they
offered for 'improvements' which would enhance their picturesque-
ness), 'Capability' Brown reigned supreme over the practice of

I   117

landscape-gardening for more than three decades until his death in 1783. His output was prodigious, and so unrestrained was his passion for 'improvements' and so drastic were his methods that one of his contemporaries said that he only hoped that he would die first so that he could see heaven before Brown had 'improved' on it.

Brown's clumps and avenues, sweeping lawns, and serpentine paths and lakes, failed to gain universal approval, however, and William Chambers, for instance, who preferred 'gardens of emotions' inspired by Salvator Rosa or the Chinese, found him vulgar and monotonous. But 'improvement', in one form or another, remained all the rage, and Walpole records how Italian the 'new face' of England was becoming as a result. Walpole's own book was one of the best of the spate of works which now appeared on the new theory of gardening and the Picturesque. The burning interest which the subject aroused can be seen from the extraordinary amount of ink spilt in the interminable controversy between those who, like Humphry Repton, remained faithful to the memory of Brown, and the rival school who objected that the latter had been more practical than Picturesque, and ought to have adhered to 'the universal principles of painting' even more closely than he did.

By that time, splendid parks with groves of choice trees and ornamental waters had become a familiar feature of the English countryside, their nobility redeeming it from mere prettiness. To quote from Walpole once again, 'Every journey is made through a succession of pictures. . . . If we have the seeds of a Claude or Gaspar among us, he must come forth.' The eighteenth-century passion to create beauty had produced the lovely synthesis of great architecture and poetic landscape, ideal forms in an ideal setting, which, in spite of its Italian inspiration, now seems to us to be so essentially English.

It did not remain entirely unique to England, however. The mania for the picturesque style of gardening, an invention of which the English were inordinately proud, spread to the continent, where it was often imitated with more enthusiasm than discrimination. Rousseau's cult of Nature had helped to pave the way. Even in France the formal Le Nôtre tradition was undermined, and Marie-Antoinette herself possessed a 'jardin anglais'. The fashion was also adopted not only in Belgium, Germany and Russia, but finally by Italy herself. Thus the ideal of Italian landscapes that had so to speak been 'made in England', returned to its land of origin, and some modern Italian towns still boast dusty patches of ground labelled 'Giardino inglese', although these are only pathetic parodies of their noble prototype.

Englishmen have exported this form of garden to more distant parts of the world as well. Examples can be found as far afield as Australia and New Zealand. In Calcutta, Singapore and Ceylon too, English landscape-architects created great gardens which required earth-moving, lake-digging and hill-making on the heroic eighteenth-century scale in order to create an attractive topography; and these relics of the imperial past are more likely to arouse the admiration of posterity than are the average examples of British colonial architecture.

In England itself, however, the golden age of landscape-gardening had passed its peak soon after the beginning of the nineteenth century. Although with Humphry Repton we are still in the enchanted world of Claude and Poussin, popular taste had at last begun to tire of vast tracts of muddy lawn, and there followed a reaction in favour of the more formal type of Italian terraced garden. Interest in the subject, moreover, was never to attain the same intensity again. But achievements of the landscape-gardeners were already there for all to see: during the hundred years between 1720 and 1820 hardly a garden had been left unaltered and the English countryside had been changed out of recognition.

Now in our own day, when generations have grown up divorced from nature, the face of England is being transformed yet once again. The fragile beauty of Arcadia is in full retreat before the ruthless onslaughts of modernity. But some of the old gardens remain. Beneath the rash of factories and pylons, the new towns and suburbs, the interminable roads and motor-cars, there still sometimes lingers a nostalgic reflection of the visions of the Italian painters.

CHAPTER 7

ROMANTIC YEARNINGS

We are all Greeks. Our laws, our literature, our religion, our arts, have their roots in Greece. But for Greece – Rome, the instructor, the conqueror, and the metropolis of our ancestors, would have spread no illumination with her arms, and we might still have been savages and idolaters.

Shelley

Italy is the place – the paradise of exiles and the retreat of Pariahs.

Shelley

The great age of the Grand Tour was brought to an end when the frontiers were closed by the Napoleonic wars. When they reopened again in 1815, Europe emerged as a very different place. Not only had political frontiers and institutions changed. Men's minds had changed too, and new frontiers were opening for the human spirit. Many of the rules and standards which had seemed all-important in the 'Age of Reason' were now eclipsed by new-born romantic enthusiasms. Freedom had become the great popular ideal: freedom in thought and emotion, freedom in life and politics. The reaction from the old classicism to this new romanticism had already begun before the end of the previous century. By now it had gathered pace, altering the nature of the traditional English ties with the civilizations of the Mediterranean. But it was not long before fresh links were formed, and the period which the historians have labelled 'the Romantic Revival' was in some respects the high summer of Greek and Italian influences in Britain.

Although there was by this time a new spirit abroad and so much would soon be changed, there was, however, no abrupt break with the past. For the English have generally tended to be incorrigible romantics in their heart of hearts, and even in the eighteenth-century heyday of classicism a man of sensibility was expected to adopt a romantic approach to the classical. Stirrings in the depths of the English subconscious coloured their feeling for classicism with romantic overtones and prepared them for the Romantic Revival. And when they now embraced the new movement, they still clung to their classical heritage none the less, as if once again seeking to have the best of both worlds.

Thus, we find classical traditions still persisting, and happily coexisting with Romanticism. Shelley, for instance, knew more Greek than Pope, and had a deeper understanding for the Greece of antiquity; whilst in architecture, to take another example, the inroads of the new imitation Gothic did not prevent most of our principal buildings aspiring to the purest of classical styles. In politics there was sometimes a similar confusion: although the French Revolution can in a sense be counted among the first fruits of the Romantic Movement, the revolutionaries themselves invoked ancient Greek examples, and their successors in the time of the Consulate felt themselves as much heirs to the virtues of republican Rome as any Whig politician might have done a generation before.

So devotion to the classical ideal survived. If people had tired of the more constricting trappings of the Augustan conventions and now rejected many of the classical disciplines, it was largely because these had come to seem to them to be an artificial barrier separating them from the true spirit of Rome and Athens. The poets and artists of the Romantic period seldom repudiated the classical tradition, but they interpreted it differently, identifying it first and foremost with the ancient Greek ideals of freedom.

It was natural for the Romantics to feel out of harmony with the realities of their time. They delighted to escape, at least in spirit, from their cold and uncongenial northern world; and their nostalgia for the past drew them towards the Middle Ages or back to the civilizations of classical antiquity. It was usually for the Greece of the golden age, rather than for ancient Rome, that the Romantics most passionately yearned. Hellas was revered as the birthplace of freedom, and of beauty and nobility in life and art. They seem to have conceived it as a kind of legendary fairy-land. It was the ideal country of their dreams; and the 'Greek Revival' became an all-embracing movement, extending far beyond the realm of architecture.

But as their romantic partiality lay with the imaginary in preference to the real, they were seldom able to feel any comparable enthusiasm for the Greece of their own day. Apart from Byron, there were few spirits bold enough to be prepared to venture into such a backward and uninviting country, which had lost its liberties so long ago and now seemed more deserving of pity than of admiration. Even when news started to come in of risings against the Turks, the factiousness of the insurgents repeatedly dashed the hopes of the philhellenes that this would mark the real beginning of Greek regeneration.

Modern Italy, on the other hand, appeared an infinitely attractive place in the eyes of this romantically-minded generation. It was far more accessible than Greece, and life there was relatively civilized and comfortable (besides being, incidentally, extraordinarily cheap). Above all, this was a land where everything – its poets, history, landscape, art – fitted into the ideal romantic pattern. So Italy inevitably became a favourite goal for English people when they flocked abroad again after the peace settlement in 1815. Two years later Byron reported that Rome was 'pestilent with English – a parcel of staring boobies, who go about gaping and wishing to be at once cheap and magnificent', and he advised anyone who was not a fool to keep away from Italy until the first ugly rush was over.

But it did not in fact turn out to be just a passing phase. Although the Grand Tour never quite reassumed its former significance, hordes of English travellers continued to head for Italy, particularly during the first two post-war decades. They included not only politicians like

Liverpool, Russell and Peel, but also a remarkable number of the leading writers, artists and architects, who believed a spell in Italy to be essential to their artistic education.

This new wave of tourists belonged to a generation which had become intensely sensitive to natural beauty and the romance of the past. Less concerned with the achievements of man than with the works of nature, they looked at Italy with different eyes to the eighteenth-century aristocrats who had established the tradition of the Grand Tour. Whereas the latter had liked to fancy themselves to be the counterpart of the ancient Romans, the young men who now toured Italy cultivating their romantic sensibilities were more likely to imagine themselves to be pilgrims treading in the footsteps of Byron's 'Childe Harold'.

By this time Italy had come back into fashion in other ways as well. She had been admired as the fountainhead of the arts ever since Reynolds had given his authority to Michelangelo and Italian painting. Gibbon's great work had meanwhile revived English interest in Italy's history: its violent drama was very much to the romantic taste and helped to awaken sympathy for the cause of Italian freedom. But Italy's literature and language returned to favour too, largely thanks to their rediscovery by the Romantic poets.

The colourful world of medieval and Renaissance Italy possessed an enormous romantic attraction. The older Italian literature could supply English writers with ready-made plots appealing to their passion for the picturesque. The Romantic generation liked much the same authors as the Elizabethans had done before them. Dante, by this time more widely known through Cary's blank-verse translations, met with particular approval, not only as a poet but also as a patriot. Thus taste had swung very far since Walpole had dismissed him as 'extravagant, absurd, disgusting'. Boccaccio had repeatedly provided a source of inspiration for English writers from Chaucer onwards; now he and the 'novelle' were popular both with the poets and with essayists like Hazlitt and Landor, whose writings helped to spread the fashionable interest for Italy. Other favourites were Tasso and Ariosto, whose romances, with their paladins and tourneys, influenced Macaulay and inspired those of Walter Scott. All these Italian writers constituted an accepted part of the English literary education. It became in fact abundantly clear that the Mediterranean world could have as powerful an appeal to the romantic as to the classical in the English temperament.

The consequences of the revolutionary transformation in men's outlook at this time extended far beyond literature and the arts, however. It was a revolt of Youth against Age, of visionary imagination against the adult intellectual. The new romantic enthusiasms included not only the old Greek ideals of freedom and democracy, but also patriotic nationalism, which the cosmopolitan eighteenth century had tended to despise as a barbarous relic of the past. All these are still very much with us today; and there are people for whom even revolution itself retains something of its glamour as the last great romantic adventure.

The ideas and emotions which emerged in the Romantic epoch continue to be a living force in other respects as well. Not only is it from them that the contemporary artist ultimately derives his cult of intense subjectivity. The rebellious spirits of our own day, who believe themselves so *avant-garde*, have more in common than they realize with the angry young men of the time of the French Revolution and of Byron, who would no doubt have sympathized with their romantic urge for self-expression and for the rejection of established values. Poets like Blake and Shelley felt no less bitterly about the crying need to change society: they were the voice of their time, knowing how to express their views with unrivalled vision and transcendental power.

For nearly two centuries the after-effects of the turmoils of Romanticism have been working themselves out. We have probably not reaped the full harvest of this extraordinary creative renewal, even now. But since the current fashion is for realism, not romanticism, and the present generation prefers to think that it has invented everything for itself, there is a tendency to overlook the Romantic parentage of a great deal that is popularly supposed to be most typically modern and new. Nowadays, therefore, the period of the Romantic Revival is principally remembered for its magnificent school of poetry.

To many of the poets who breathed the hopes of the new century, the Mediterranean legacy meant as much as it had to the Elizabethans in that other brilliant age of English verse. It is true that much else besides the Mediterranean world contributed to the stimulation of their poetic genius. The other main influence was the romanticism of Goethe's Germany. But in one respect at least, it may have been less valuable. For only the classical Mediterranean tradition was capable of providing the style and discipline to restrain the English Romantics from allowing themselves to be carried away by the emotional excesses to which the romantic temperament is so frequently prone.

The case of Shelley affords a particularly revealing illustration of the role which Greece and Italy could play for a Romantic poet. Like so many of his contemporaries, Shelley was inspired by a passionate enthusiasm for the Mediterranean world and its literature. But if Greece and Italy were both intensely important to him, it was in quite different ways. Ancient Greece provided his imagination with an ideal vision of perfection. But whilst he worshipped Hellas from afar, Italy could give him the direct sensual experience of a new world. It was a real country which he came to know and love, and his adopted home during the last four years of his life at the time he was composing so much of his greatest poetry.

Shelley was only twenty-six when, in 1818, he decided to leave England for abroad. The immediate reason seems to have been his ill-health: like many other northerners before and since, he placed his hopes on the sunshine of the Mediterranean to set him right. There was also Mary Shelley's anxiety to bring Byron's illegitimate daughter, Allegra Clairmont, to her father in Venice. But there were other, far more fundamental motives. Shelley was speaking from personal experience when he afterwards said, in writing of Byron, 'You cannot conceive the excessive violence with which the English of a certain class detest those whose conduct and opinions are not in accord with theirs.'

This was not merely Byron's problem; Shelley was equally maladjusted and had to face it too. Respectable Englishmen similarly condemned him as 'mad, bad and dangerous to know'. His private life was regarded as hardly less shocking than Byron's, and his opinions, tame though they may seem to us today, more outrageous still. Society was not likely to forgive him for breaking the code of his class, and expatriation must have appeared to him the only hope of regaining his peace of spirit. Like Byron, he ultimately found a haven in Italy; and one of the most precious services which that country has rendered to English literature is to have given these exiled poets renewed possibilities to fulfil their genius.

The revelation of the Mediterranean world came as a tremendously exciting experience for Shelley. The first impressions of this beauty-intoxicated young poet are recorded in his letters, where he writes ecstatically of the 'loveliness of the earth and the serenity of the sky'. These, he said, were things on which he depended 'for life; for in the smoke of cities, and the tumult of human kind, and the chilling fogs and rain of our country, I can hardly be said to live.' 'Health, competence, tranquillity – all these Italy permits and England takes away.' Shelley's temperament was far too mercurial for such euphoria to last, but although he might sometimes become homesick for England and would always remain one of the most essentially English of poets, he never left Italy again and it was there that his poetry achieved its fullest flowering.

The poetic harvest of Shelley's last years shows how eagerly his ardent mind and sensitivity responded to his new surroundings. Not only was his imagery enriched by his experiences, as when the Venetian gondolas evoked the lovely simile 'moths of which a coffin might have been the chrysalis'. The spate of splendid verse shows how much his creative powers were now enhanced. As Mary Shelley observed, 'the charm of the Rome climate helped to clothe his thoughts in greater beauty than they had ever worn before.' But it is Shelley's own words in the preface of *Prometheus Unbound* that best express the debt which he felt he owed to the Italian enchantment. 'This poem', he explains, 'was chiefly written upon the mountainous ruins of the Baths of Caracalla, among the flowery glades, and thickets of odoriferous blossoming trees. . . . The bright blue sky of Rome, and the effect of the vigorous awakening spring in that divinest climate, and the new life with which it drenches the spirits even to intoxication, were the inspiration of this drama.'

Scarcely more than fifty years before another English writer had similarly conceived a masterpiece amongst the ancient ruins of Rome. But it had been of a significantly different character. As Gilbert Highet has pointed out, Gibbon stood at the end of an epoch and looked backwards, writing the sober obituary of a bygone age; whereas Shelley, at the beginning of a new and hopeful century, composed an exhilarating paean of praise to a beauty perpetually reborn, as though looking forward to the day when

> The world's great age begins anew,
> The golden years return. . . .

Nature-worship came easily to romantics like Shelley, and Italy brought to fruition his special gift of clothing Nature with emotional and symbolic significance. The splendid visual imagery of a poem like his 'Lines Written among the Euganean Hills' proves how well the beauty of Italy could inspire him. On the other hand, the results were not always equally happy when he turned to Italian history and politics for his themes, as in 'The Cenci' or his 'Ode to Naples'.

Apart from the Italian scene, the most valuable stimulus which Shelley received from Italy was through her literature. Dante he admired especially, considering him to surpass all other poets except Shakespeare in his 'exquisite tenderness, sensibility and ideal beauty'. One of his first letters after he reached Italy gives a characteristic glimpse of Shelley in Milan cathedral, reading Dante 'in a solitary spot among the aisles'; and he became enthralled by the *Inferno*, which he and Mary Shelley used to read aloud to one another.

The poet who claimed poets to be 'the unacknowledged legislators of the world' felt that in Dante he had discovered a kindred spirit, attaching the same supreme importance to the sublime role which poetry should play. Out of this fundamentally common approach came a similar kind of symbolism and imagery, even though Shelley could never hope to equal Dante's intellectual power, and was too often inclined to content himself with wordy emotional generalities. His

'Ode to the West Wind', written on the banks of the Arno, contains a haunting echo of the *Inferno* in its description of whirling leaves 'like ghosts from an enchanter fleeing'. His admiration for Dante's style and metre led him to imitate them in this and other poems, as well as in his translation from the *Commedia*.

More important than any such stylistic influences, Dante encouraged Shelley to arrive at his conception of the ideal spiritual love of woman which could link man with the divinity. He felt the idealism of his love for Emilia Viviani, the young daughter of the Governor of Pisa, to be of the same essence as Dante's love for Beatrice; and when he celebrated his last grand passion in 'Epipsychidion', he prefaced this Platonic rhapsody with what he called 'an almost literal translation' from Dante.

Petrarch was another Italian poet who had excelled at writing of the sublime themes of love and death with a mystical ecstasy very close to Shelley's own, and Shelley pointed to Petrarch's sonnets, many of which he knew by heart, as an illustration of how poetry ought to contribute to the moral improvement of mankind. The last of his major poems, 'The Triumph of Life', in Petrarchan tercets, is essentially a homage to Petrarch and to Dante. In this unfinished work Shelley seems to be reaching out beyond his dreams of an impossible millennium, to something a little nearer to the kind of Olympian detachment which was part of Dante's greatness.

But this is Shelley's only important poem where the main literary influences are unmistakably Italian. Much as he loved his favourite Italian authors, he always remained a Greek at heart. He called the Greeks 'our masters and creators, the gods whom we should worship'. For the Romantic poets, classical Greece was an exquisite but ill-defined mirage, sufficiently nebulous to allow each of them to shape it after the image of his own fantasy. In Shelley's case, it represented the noblest embodiment of those ideals of freedom and beauty which were the ruling passion of his life and the inspiration of his poetry. So fervent was his admiration for everything Greek that, as his 'Hellas' shows, he did not entirely despair even of contemporary Greece.

Always a tremendous reader, and with a command of the two

classical languages typical of the well-educated man of his time, year after year Shelley read and re-read Homer and the other Greek classics until they coloured his whole philosophy. He translated the *Symposium*, and the abstract artistic, political and religious ideas which so enthralled him were strongly marked by his Platonism (although his vague and sentimental optimism did not in fact have very much in common with Plato's ethical austerity). He was fascinated by Greek mythology, using it as a vehicle for expressing his own high-flown theories about the future of humanity, and his major metaphysical poem, 'Prometheus Unbound', was conceived as a sequel to the *Prometheus Bound* of Aeschylus.

Greek literature always remained Shelley's constant companion, and when he met his death by drowning in the Gulf of Lerici, his Sophocles was one of the two books afterwards found in the pocket of his jacket. The second was the poems of that other devout lover of ancient Greece, John Keats, whose own death had moved Shelley to a pastoral lament reminiscent of the dirges which Greek bucolic poets used to compose for Adonis in olden times.

Keats himself had all his life pined for the warm South. 'Who would live', he once wrote from Devon, 'in the region of Mists, Game Laws, Indemnity Bills etc., when there is such a place as Italy?' He never managed to get there until he knew that death was at his elbow, and the last few months in Rome were what he called his 'posthumous life'. But in a sense that hardly mattered; for in his extraordinarily vivid imagination, he had so often travelled in these 'realms of gold' that the Mediterranean world could become almost as real to him as it was to Shelley, who knew it so well at first hand.

Keats's sources of inspiration were generally less literary than Shelley's. His knowledge of Italian literature was more superficial and he never mastered the language. But he felt a similar admiration for Dante, whom he read in Cary's translation, and if his 'Endymion' is a testimony to his neo-Platonism, 'Hyperion' shows his close study of the *Purgatorio*. He found something else in Dante which especially affected him. The story of Paolo and Francesca seemed as poignant as his own star-crossed love for Fanny Brawne: he gave her a copy of the fifth canto of the *Inferno*, and on its fly-leaf she inscribed the 'Bright Star' sonnet he had composed for her.

But it was Greece and Greek poetry that moved him most. Even though he might sometimes use medieval Italian themes, as in his 'Isabella', for Keats as for Shelley the classical past had the more powerful attraction, because it appeared to represent a higher order of nobility and greatness. There were admittedly wide gaps in his knowledge of Greece, and he was never capable of organizing his longer poems with the clarity of the Greek authors. But he fell under the spell of the enchanted world of the gods and heroes of mythology. His choice of subjects tells its own story – Hyperion, Endymion, a Grecian Urn, Lamia and the odes to Apollo. He was enamoured of the Greek spirit, which he described as 'the Religion of the Beautiful, the Religion of Joy'. This was the purer air, the 'pure serene', for which his spirit always yearned with quivering intensity.

Many other poets have felt the influence of Greek and Italian thought and literature, but none of them has probably owed so much as Keats to Greek sculpture and Italian painting. Beauty in all its various forms appealed to him and he had an overwhelming sense of visual beauty. The visual arts stimulated his all-embracing imagination, enriching his response to the world of nature. He would often speak of his own poetry in terms of painting. He had a painter's eye, resembling the Elizabethan poets in his delight in word-pictures, in which he clothed splendid pictorial images in equally splendid verse.

Sometimes these poetic descriptions can be related to actual Italian paintings, which he would generally have known from the print collections of his artist friends like Benjamin Haydon. There seems no question, for instance, that his description of Autumn, 'sitting careless on a granary floor' with 'hair soft-lifted by the winnowing wind', derives from Giulio Romano's picture of the sleeping Psyche. Another fascinating example of the perennial Mediterranean legacy is the way Keats responded to the inspiration of Titian's *Bacchus and Ariadne*, which had in its turn been inspired by the Greek myths as interpreted by Ovid and the Renaissance poets. The two painters whose pictures particularly affected his poetic vision, however, were Poussin, the great interpreter of the old legends which meant so much to Keats, and Claude, whose *Enchanted Castle* is thought to have evoked the lovely image of 'magic casements, opening on the foam of perilous seas, in faery lands forlorn', in his 'Ode to a Nightingale'.

Greek art was bound to have a very special significance for an artist so fervently absorbed by the cult of beauty, and there can be little doubt that the most overwhelming of Keats's artistic experiences was his sight of the marbles from the Parthenon. In his first flush of enthusiasm he composed his sonnet 'On Seeing the Elgin Marbles', and he afterwards returned again and again to the British Museum, where he would sit gazing at them for hours, enraptured. For this young poet who had never visited the Mediterranean, they revealed the vision of a new world, even more exhilarating, perhaps, than his first discovery of Homer in Chapman's noble version of the *Iliad*.

'Hyperion' shows how powerfully the Elgin Marbles moved Keats's imagination. So does the 'Grecian Urn', even though this sonnet in which he probably came nearest to achieving his ideal of Greek perfection, may not have been inspired by any specific 'Attic shape', and his ideas seem also to have owed something to Claude's *Sacrifice to Apollo*, and to the articles which Haydon was publishing on Raphael's cartoon, *The Sacrifice at Lystra*. The whole concept of the poem is essentially, however, a profession of Keats's passionate belief in the immortal ideals of Greek art, where beauty could express a higher truth.

Coleridge is yet another of the Romantic poets who felt the fascination of the Mediterranean world. His studies of the Italian Renaissance poets helped him to polish his technique: like them, he was careful to vary his metres, and he invoked the example of Dante in support of his own attempts to bring the artificial language of poetry nearer to ordinary speech. But nowadays he is seldom remembered for his 'Garden of Boccaccio' or his devotion to Giordano Bruno, and his most famous works bear the imprint less of Italy than of Greece or still more distant lands. Critics will probably always differ over the exact interpretation of those splendidly mysterious poems, but it is generally accepted that an element of Orphism runs through much of

21 Claude's *Aeneas at Delos* (*see page 97*)

22 Claude's *Embarkation of the Queen of Sheba* (see page 102)

23 Turner's *Dido Build-ing Carthage* (see page 102)

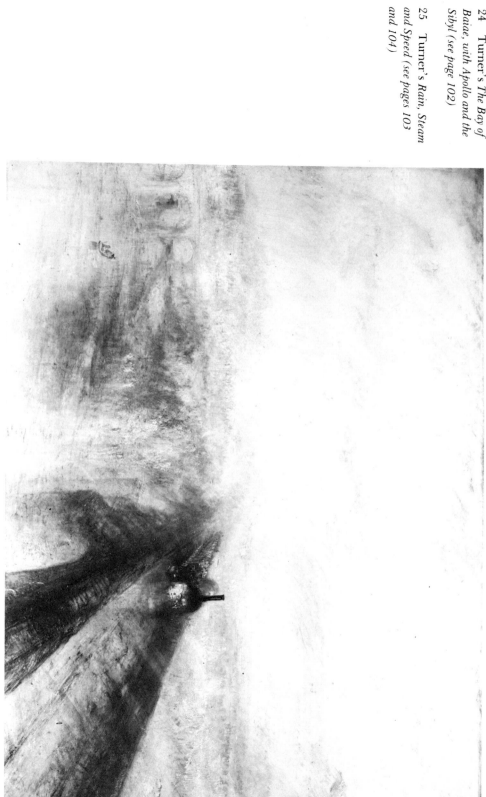

24 Turner's *The Bay of Baiae, with Apollo and the Sibyl (see page 102)*

25 Turner's *Rain, Steam and Speed (see pages 103 and 104)*

Two painters' impressions of Englishmen's eighteenth-century landscapes. Turner's *Petworth Park*

27 Constable's *Wivenhoe Park, Essex*

28 Victorian tourists at Venice (*see page 142*)

the mythical imagery of 'Kubla Khan', where the sacred river Alph can probably be identified with Lethe, and that the *Odyssey* may supply a clue to the riddles of his 'Ancient Mariner'. Greek philosophy, Homer and the neo-Platonists fed the daydreams of this great romantic dreamer whose poetry speaks the symbolic language of their ageless wisdom.

Wordsworth, on the other hand, stood closer to Italy than to Greece, even though what is possibly his finest poem, the 'Intimations of Immortality', has overtones of Platonism. He had learnt Italian and translated Italian poetry whilst he was still at Cambridge, and his studies of Petrarch and other Italian precedents influenced his own development of the sonnet form. One of the best of his sonnets was provoked by the extinction of the Venetian Republic at the hands of Napoleon, for although he did not know the country well (he had visited Como on an undergraduate walking-tour but failed to get to Italy again until he was middle-aged), his essentially insular loyalties did not inhibit him from sharing the warm sympathy felt by so many English liberals and writers for the cause of Italian liberty.

More than any other poet, however, it is Lord Byron who is the romantic figure that most Englishmen and practically all foreigners particularly associate with Greece and Italy and their struggle for freedom. Not that his efforts to help the Greeks and Italians ever came to very much. Nor, for that matter, do we now consider him to be the better poet, even if he possessed a more universal appeal than those whose poetry was more personal and more magical. But he had a unique capacity for taking the centre of the stage and keeping it. His extraordinary personality caught the imagination of Europe in a way that no other Englishman's had ever done before, giving a legendary significance to everything he did.

Although European opinion insisted on regarding him as the incarnation of romanticism, Byron was always reluctant to allow himself to be identified with the other romantics of his time, and his attitude towards Greece and Italy was characteristically more ambivalent than theirs. Always more interested in the present, he would never have admitted to the respectful reverence of a Shelley or a Keats towards the classical past. Nor did he wish it to be supposed that he shared the popular craze for sights and scenery: moonlight and fine views were, he once remarked, dangerously conducive to the sort of sentimentality which he held in horror. There was certainly nothing solemn about his approach to antiquities, and he detested what he called 'antiquarian twaddle'. He scratched his name on the marble of Sounion like any vulgar tourist, and when first shown the Parthenon, all he could find to say was that it put him in mind of the Mansion House. But we can never be entirely sure of Byron's true feelings; he was an *enfant terrible* who loved to tease, and flippancy was a favourite weapon to disguise his emotions. However much he affected to despise such things, the Mediterranean scene certainly enriched his poetic imagery; and as is evident from his musings in *Childe Harold* on the vanished glories of Rome, the time would come when he could take a melancholy pleasure in ruins, which seemed to symbolize his own devastated soul.

In any event, the genuineness of Byron's passionate sentiments for Greece can hardly be disputed. It had been there that he found his first real poetic inspiration. He was barely twenty-one when he embarked on a Grand Tour in the highest romantic style, a leisurely pilgrimage full of every kind of picturesque adventure. There were rides through the mountains of Albania with tribesmen whose primitive passions and savage heroism were after his own heart; meetings with that formidable old ruffian, Ali Pasha; Athens, where he could find handsome youths and girls appealing to his catholic tastes; his swim across the Hellespont in the track of Leander; a visit to the Turkish Sultan, and the fabulous spectacle of Constantinople; not to mention a host of other excitements, including a shipwreck and a brush with pirates in the Aegean. After such heady stuff, life could never be quite the same again for an impressionable young romantic like Byron. In Greece he had discovered his spiritual home: the spiritual home of both Childe Harold and Don Juan. There he had felt exhilaratingly free and in his element. Henceforth, England, in contrast, was bound to seem a little drab.

Besides a weird assortment of souvenirs, including an Albanian costume and a variety of marbles, tortoises and skulls, Byron brought back from Greece the first two cantos of *Childe Harold's Pilgrimage*. This picaresque epic made him famous overnight. Written under the inspiration of his travels, it provided a sort of Grand Tour for armchair travellers which enlarged the horizon of the European imagination. But these were only the first fruits of his 'Wanderjahre'. For he also returned with countless enchanted memories from which his essentially descriptive talents could draw themes and imagery for future poems, where he would often sing nostalgically of the lands of the Aegean, with 'the bluest of all waves and the brightest of all skies'.

Five years later Byron was back in the South once again, but this time in very different circumstances. He had won the acclaim of the whole of Europe as the hero and poet of the age. But his social eclipse had been as spectacular as his meteoric rise to fame. In 1816, when scandal had caught up with him, he shook the dust of England off his feet for ever, settling in Italy, where he was to remain until he embarked on his last journey to Greece. Whilst Byron appears to have had his reservations about the contemporary enthusiasm for the romanticism of the country, life in Italy at least offered the great attraction of enabling him to escape from what he felt to be the nightmare of English cant and hypocrisy.

Venice, where he chose to pass most of his time after his first arrival, seemed to him just the place. There, he could flout English conventions to his heart's content, and enjoy the privacy and freedom from responsibility after which he had always hankered. The Byronic temperament flourishes on emotional and sensual excitement, and the hectic round of Venetian pleasures brought his literary genius to its highest pitch. It was during this period that he wrote the first part of his *Don Juan*, the light-hearted, witty satire in which his gifts found their happiest expression. This poem owed something else to Italy too, for Byron borrowed the mock-heroic style and octave metre of the Italian Renaissance writers, thus introducing into English Romantic literature the only important new trend directly derived from Italy.

After his three profligate Venetian years, it becomes more difficult to identify what other significant stimulus Byron's genius was able to derive from his time in Italy, even though he spent most of his adult life there, living so long among the Italians that he came to feel, he said, 'more for them as a nation than for any other in existence'. Doubtless, his affair with Teresa Guiccioli could bring him unaccustomed peace of mind for a while; but Byron was not made for domesticity, and his talents were of a kind that thrived better on stimulants than on sedatives. Certainly, his Ravenna period was extremely productive; many of his poems had Italian themes, with writers such as Dante and Alfieri making an important contribution. His poetry seldom, however, again achieved the same happy spontaneity as it had done in Venice.

Nor did Italy provide much scope for Byron's self-elected role of the artist as romantic hero. Works like *Marino Faliero* and his 'Ode to Venice' are evidence that his sympathy for the cause of Italian freedom was genuine enough: he called it 'the very poetry of politics', and when concluding *Childe Harold* he praised the Italians for their 'longing after immortality – the immortality of independence'. But once he had discovered the futility of his young friends in the Carbonari who were content merely to play at revolution, he soon grew tired of dabbling in their amateurish conspiracies.

For a time he managed to resign himself to his placid existence in provincial Italian society. But a life offering so little of the novelty and excitement for which his restless nature craved was in the long run bound to pall. His heart had, he wryly lamented, 'become as grey as his head', and for a man who set such store by his romantic legend, it was scarcely conceivable that everything should be allowed to end in the anti-climax of a humdrum bourgeois middle age. Feeling that it was high time to resume his heroic pose, the call of Greece proved irresistible. By joining in her fight for freedom, he hoped against hope to recapture something of his carefree youth, or at least to refurbish his romantic reputation. As if to emphasize the theatricality of the gesture, he equipped himself for his escapade with an elaborately picturesque uniform, complete with a Homeric helmet of his own design. Always a determined fatalist, he seems to have sensed, however, that he was destined never to return.

As we know, Byron's Greek expedition turned out a miserable fiasco: he failed to see any fighting against the Turks and the circumstances of his death in the squalor of Missolonghi were pathetically inglorious. None the less, his gamble for immortality paid off. Greece, the country he always loved above all others, and the inspiration of so much of his poetry, had now done him a last service. She had provided the opportunity for a fitting finale to the man who had boasted in *Don Juan*:

> . . . plain, sworn, downright detestation
> Of every despotism in every nation.

He had ended on a note hardly, it is true, of romantic heroism, but only of high pathos. But by yet one last Byronic paradox, his pathetic failure stirred the imagination of the age better than success, consecrating his legend as the hero of liberty and national freedom. No other English poet has ever exercised such a far-reaching influence on European literature and thought; and none probably owed so much, in such a wide variety of different ways, to the world of the Mediterranean.

CHAPTER 8

VICTORIANA

Three of the most celebrated Romantic poets died young, and within a very few years of each other: Keats in 1821, Shelley in 1822 and Byron two years later. The Romantic Movement had already passed its peak by the time Queen Victoria came to the throne in 1837. Soon there would be a very different spirit in England and although some Romantic tendencies survived, it was sentiment and realism that became the dominant notes in art and literature.

The end of High Romanticism also marks the close of the most important chapters in the long history of this country's cultural relationship with Italy. Whilst Italian influences were still by no means entirely eclipsed, their imprint on British civilization no longer presented such a clear and coherent picture. Henceforth the pattern becomes more blurred. Nor was there any longer the same reverence for Italian art and architecture simply because they were Italian. Italy was never again to mean quite so much to the British as she had during the first three centuries since the beginning of the Elizabethan Renaissance.

The previous generation's enthusiasm for Italy had, after all, been rather a romantic affair. A reaction inevitably set in once the Romantic tide began to ebb. The more matter-of-fact Victorians did not take long to discover that the place was not quite the earthly paradise that

Romantic poets had made it out to be, and contained not only moonlit ruins, but squalor and mosquitoes as well. And there were other, more fundamental reasons why the generation of Dickens could not be expected to idealize Italy in the way that Keats and Shelley had done. The moral climate in Victorian England had changed a great deal since the days of the Grand Tour and the free-thinking of Gibbon. Christianity had swept back in the flood-tide of Evangelicalism, and when eyes are fixed on celestial Grace, earthly graces are apt to be forgotten. Life was real, life was earnest; and it was a sign of the times when the word 'dilettante', instead of being a flattering term to describe a person fortunate enough to be capable of appreciating the finer things in life, came to mean a mere trifler. Lord Byron was an awful example of what such frivolity could do to the morals of a gentleman: far better, therefore, the clean-limbed young Englishman on a walking-tour amongst the English lakes.

The brash and thriving new England of the Industrial Revolution, where middle-class insularity had supplanted the cosmopolitan aristocratic culture of the previous century, could hardly feel much affinity with people like the Italians who appeared so distressingly lacking in any desire to relinquish the past and join in the march of progress of the modern world. Complacently self-sufficient and preoccupied with the present, the Victorians were less inclined to envy Italy for her ancient culture than to pity her for her backwardness.

Now it was the turn of France and particularly of Germany to come into fashion. The new Germany was regarded as a commendably progressive country, and the Germans possessed precisely the kind of qualities which the Victorians most admired. Not only were they virtuous, practical and efficient. They were intellectual and artistic as well, and Goethe and Beethoven had shown that Germany could produce writers and musicians immeasurably more gifted than any of their Italian contemporaries.

But even when the intellectual fascination of Germany captured English minds, Italy did not altogether lose her hold on the English imagination. Many of the finer spirits still remained faithful to the South. Out of tune with the ugly materialism which had produced the

England of William Blake's 'dark Satanic mills', they looked nostalgically towards the Mediterranean where the older civilizations seemed
to have succeeded in retaining a more gracious way of life, based on
the kind of spiritual values they themselves were so anxious to preserve.
But to the majority of the Victorians, however, this only smacked of
false romanticism, and in their eyes, the decadence of modern Italy
and Greece appeared even more deplorable by contrast with these
countries' glorious past.

But although Italy was now losing some of her former glamour and
cultural prestige for most English people, she was, on the other hand,
by this time starting to enlist their political sympathies, with the
result that new ties eventually developed which went some way to
offset the loosening of the old. The Napoleonic wars had involved
Britain more closely in Mediterranean affairs, and the peace settlement
left Malta and the protectorate of the Ionian Islands in British hands.
(One curious legacy of that period is the Order of St Michael and
St George, originally established by the Prince Regent in 1818 to
reward the more deserving of his new subjects in these recently
acquired possessions but nowadays mainly given to British diplomats.)
Their political stake in the Mediterranean, the 'life-line to India',
helped to awaken the sympathetic interest of the English in the
struggles of the Greeks and Italians to liberate their countries from
foreign rule. And sentiment played an important role as well, for
English liberals were eager to see other nations enjoy the much-vaunted
British freedom.

But although Byron could no longer have taunted the Italians with
tamely submitting to foreign domination, the revolutionaries still
often disillusioned their English friends by the way they allowed their
efforts to peter out in some futile fiasco. It was not until Garibaldi
and Cavour had redeemed them from their rather comic-opera
reputation that they became entirely respectable in Victorian eyes, and
the passionate pro-Italian propaganda of the Brownings and their circle
could at last bear fruit. By 1859, enthusiasm for the Italian cause
reached such a pitch that it even helped change the course of English
politics, for it was a factor in the fall of the Tory government which

brought back into office Lord Palmerston and Lord John Russell.

The Italophil sentiments of English liberals seem generally to have been cultural in origin, and if Gladstone, for instance, felt such strong sympathy for Italy, it was partially because of his life-long passion for her literature. Dante and Homer were his gods, and in his old age he declared with characteristic sententiousness that it had been to the school of Dante that he owed 'a great part of the mental provision' for his 'journey of human life'.

Apart from politics, however, there was another development which helped to sustain English interest in Italy. The dawn of the railway age in the 1830s opened a new era of foreign travel, and a few years later mass tourism was pioneered by the enterprising Baptist preacher, Thomas Cook. It was the railway, Dickens's 'triumphant monster', that gave the *coup de grâce* to the Grand Tour. European travel ceased to be a luxury which only the rich and leisured upper classes could afford. A trip to Italy now became well within the reach of the bourgeoisie, who by this time had money to spare and a thirst for self-improvement.

The age of the first railways was also the age of the first guide-books. The new generation of tourists were in far more of a hurry, and coming from a less cultivated and sophisticated world than the 'grand tourists' of the past, they mistrusted their own taste and needed some reliable authority to tell them what they ought properly to admire. Herr Baedeker, the quintessence of Teutonic thoroughness and accuracy, and Mr Murray (the first of whose famous *Handbooks* was published in 1836) provided the answer to their problem, and those of them who wanted something more ambitious did not have long to wait before they were able to supplement their instruction from authors like John Ruskin, J. A. Symonds and Augustus Hare.

Italy, with her romantic associations and wealth of historic monuments, still retained her place amongst Europe's most popular tourist attractions. This was the age of the Victorian paterfamilias, grossly overdressed for the Italian climate, steering his brood through the hot and crowded streets of Rome and Florence, back to their 'pensione' after an improving morning in the museums; eager maiden ladies clutching their Baedekers and Ruskins, grimly determined not to miss any of the 'sights'; earnest scholars intent on swotting-up Italian art and history; and there were also, of course, countless honeymoon couples, for then, as always, Italy was a favourite with lovers.

This sentimental enthusiasm for Italy seldom extended to her inhabitants, however. The Victorians were shocked by the failure of the Italians to show any proper respect for the right principles of behaviour, hygiene or efficiency. Worse still, these feckless and benighted people seemed blissfully unconscious of their shortcomings and perfectly happy to go on as they were. Matthew Arnold voiced the reaction of high-minded Victorian morality in deploring the Italian lack of 'back-bone, serious energy and the power of honest work'.

Even a man like Ruskin, who was passionately fond of Italy in his own way, could express himself with extraordinary venom on the subject. He found the Italians hopelessly vicious; they were, he told his father, like 'Yorick's skull with the worms in it – nothing left of humanity but the smell'. Italy might, indeed, have been one of the countries in the Victorian hymn, where 'every prospect pleases and only man is vile'. Not quite 'only man', perhaps, for there were also frequent complaints about the voracity of the insects. The latter were no respecters of persons, and Cardinal Newman wrote a lurid description of his encounter with that redoubtable beast, the Sicilian flea.

Despite their appetite for knowledge and their genuine appreciation of beauty, the Victorians were in fact far too insular to make ideal travellers, apart from being in much too great a hurry. Smugly confident of their English superiority to lesser breeds like the Latins and damned if they'd conform to foreign ways, they assumed that because foreigners so obstinately insisted on being different, they could not possibly have anything to learn from them. Their inability ever to forget their prejudices and say 'vive la différence' must have made them miss half the fun. Even the numerous writers and artists who settled in Italy usually remained equally self-sufficient, looking on the country as a picturesque museum and taking so little interest in its people and problems that they might just as well have been living in Bath or Birmingham, instead of Florence or Fiesole.

Fortunately, there were a few honourable exceptions, particularly among the literary coterie living in Florence, a place now becoming very fashionable with English visitors, including even Queen Victoria herself. One of the most famous of these 'Anglo-Florentines' was Elizabeth Barrett Browning, whose warm feminine enthusiasm embraced everything Italian, even the much maligned Italians themselves. She had arrived in Italy soon after her clandestine marriage to Robert, and this smiling Mediterranean country, where everything was such an utter contrast to the lonely seclusion of her London sick-room, provided the perfect background for her romantic idyll. Her new-found happiness helped to make this a productive period for her poetry, and some of her best work, including *Sonnets from the Portuguese*, was written at her Florentine home, the Casa Guidi, or in the peaceful surroundings of Bagni di Lucca.

Many of her most lyrical poems were directly inspired by Italy and the struggles of the Risorgimento. She had been brought up on ideals of liberty and on the classics. As a child she dreamed of dressing up as a man and joining Byron to fight in Greece, and when she was only fourteen she wrote and published an epic on the battle of Marathon. Now that she found herself in a country striving to cast off centuries of foreign oppression, she became the self-appointed muse of the Italian cause. Her generous emotions were so ardently engaged in the high hopes and bitter disappointments of the struggle that the shock of Cavour's sudden death played a part in undermining her failing health. When she died soon afterwards in Florence in 1861, the last words she wrote were 'May God save Italy'.

The Italian sympathies of Robert Browning were by comparison pitched in a lower key. His was a cooler temperament and although he spent so much of his life in Italy, he always remained intrinsically a middle-class Victorian Englishman, whose 'Oh, to be in England' in his *Home Thoughts from Abroad* is likely to have been a genuine 'cri de coeur'. Years later, when he was back in London and basking in the social success which his vanity found it so difficult to resist, he would confess that his 'liking for Italy' had been a 'selfish one, – I felt alone with my own soul there'.

But much as Browning's genius may have needed the kind of solitude which Italy could give him, this was by no means his only debt to the country of his adoption. On another occasion he declared 'Italy was my university'; and this had in fact been true ever since his student days when he was reading Dante and Petrarch with his tutor Angelo Cerutti, one of the many Italian exiles working in England. It was not merely during his years in Italy that he was fascinated by Italian subjects and literature. 'Sordello' and 'Pippa Passes' had been written before he went to live there, and after his return to England he wrote *The Ring and the Book*, which may be described as eleven different versions of a Roman murder case he had come across in a book picked up on a second-hand bookstall in Florence.

Whereas Elizabeth was passionately concerned with the politics of the present, it would, on the other hand, be the Italy of the past which captured Robert's own imagination. Gothic romance enjoyed considerable popularity with many nineteenth-century writers: for Browning, however, medieval Italy served primarily as an appropriate setting for the exposition of his religious theories, just as he used Renaissance Italy to do the same for his humanistic values.

Many of the Victorian intelligentsia besides the Brownings found their way to Florence, which Arnold Bennett called 'the ideal place to write a novel'. Landor spent much of his life there. George Eliot came to collect material for *Romola*; Swinburne (who spoke of Italy as 'my second mother-country') for his *Song of Italy*. Anthony Trollope sometimes went to stay at his brother's Tuscan villa; whilst Layard, the archaeologist and ambassador, had a Florentine upbringing and learnt to have a genuine feeling for the Italians. There were some, like Ruskin, for whom Venice had the greater attraction; whereas it was in Rome that Thackeray wrote *The Rose and the Ring*, and a little later southern Italy was to inspire George Gissing's sensitive and scholarly *By the Ionian Sea*. Hazlitt, Scott, Dickens, Macaulay, Mrs Gaskell, Bulwer Lytton, Walter Pater and Meredith are among the numerous names which could be cited to show how few of the famous literary figures of the period escaped the influence of Italy.

In many cases, such writers felt drawn to Mediterranean culture,

particularly in its classical form, mainly because of their disenchantment with the crass materialism of their own times. Their revulsion
against the philistines and barbarians of Victorian England sent them
back to what Matthew Arnold called the 'sweetness and light' of
ancient Greece; like Wordsworth, they yearned to 'have sight of
Proteus rising from the sea'.

One notable example of this escapist longing for antiquity is the
great classicist, Walter Savage Landor. Although in his old age he
began his famous quatrain with the line 'I strove with none, for none
was worth my strife', in reality he was an exceedingly prickly person,
who managed to quarrel with practically everybody, even including
his harmless Florentine neighbours. As an artist, however, Landor
lived in a remote world of his own, shared with the classics and his
favourite Italian authors such as Dante and Boccaccio, with whom he
peopled his *Imaginary Conversations*. Much of his work has an Italian
background, breathing the spirit of a rather mannered Renaissance;
and, like so many artists of his day, he preferred to lose himself
in nostalgic daydreams of bygone times rather than face the uncongenial
problems of his own age.

Tennyson was equally typical of his generation in his classical and
Italian scholarship, and in a loyalty to the ancients that never wavered.
For some of his finest poems, such as 'Ulysses', he went to the classics
for his subject or his framework; and at moments he could write with
the warm sweetness of Theocritus, or in an elegiac Virgilian strain,
with a similar majestic sense of the past. In contrast to most of the
other poets of his time, Tennyson seems to have felt more affinity with
Rome than Greece. But even such a fervent Hellenist as Swinburne,
the poet of Greek and Italian liberty, saturated though he was in the
drama and poetry of Greece, could not help remaining essentially
un-Greek in his florid style and personality, and it is only in his
'Atalanta in Calydon' that he manages to recapture something of the
authentic Greek spirit.

The Hellenism which the Victorian poets inherited from the
Romantic Movement was, in fact, seldom more than an escapist
refuge, and the classical themes and images with which they loved to

ornament their work were all too often merely an affectation, the decorative trappings of an outworn cult. The gulf between the Mediterranean world and the harsh realities of nineteenth-century England was now too wide, and ancient Greece could no longer provide an ideal pattern of life as she had done for a poet like Shelley in the brighter, more confident morning of this second Greek Renaissance. Nostalgic withdrawal from the present into an idealized antiquity which was losing its deeper meaning, led in the end to the sterile aestheticism of art for art's sake; and Oscar Wilde's apophthegm 'Nothing succeeds like excess' might serve to sum up the final bankruptcy of the Romantic creed.

The Victorian age also saw a gradual decline in the influence of Italian music here. For a time, however, Italian opera, which had been given a fillip by Rossini's immensely successful visit in 1824, remained very much the fashion, and opera-going played a highly important part in the life of Victorian society. Verdi now emerged as a towering figure, and Puccini was later to enjoy considerable popularity in England. The remarkable vitality of the Italian opera seems also to have owed a good deal to the brilliance of the Italian singers. It had become part of a polite education to learn to sing in Italian; and even Queen Victoria had her Italian singing-teacher. Most of the leading singers went to Italy to study. So did composers like Michael Balfe and Sir Henry Bishop. The latter was the first Englishman to write music specifically for the ballet – a form of art which came into vogue here in the 1830s, following the London appearances of the great Romantic ballerinas Marie Taglioni and Fanny Elssler. Nevertheless, by mid-Victorian times, the dominance of Italy was already being seriously challenged, largely as a consequence of the predilection of the middle classes for German symphony. Italian opera still drew the aristocracy to the Haymarket, however, and it was not until 1892 that the 'Royal Italian Opera' changed its name to the 'Royal Opera', *tout court*. But by then Wagner had triumphed in England, and Italian music had finally lost its ascendency.

In the English visual arts too, the time-honoured supremacy of the classical Mediterranean tradition was on the wane, and this was something of a twilight age. There were still quantities of British painters and sculptors in the little studios round the Piazza di Spagna, which was always so packed with visitors that it would sometimes be described as 'a piece of England dropped upon the soil of Italy'. But the Italian training had ceased to have the same importance, for although academicians like Lord Leighton, who himself worked many years in Rome, strove to keep classicism alive, Victorian taste was turning increasingly towards the Gothic and the medieval. By this time, therefore, the English looked to Italy for inspiration of a different kind than before, and it was chiefly through the paintings of the Pre-Raphaelites and the writings of John Ruskin, both of which made their contribution to the new medievalist fashion, that Mediterranean influences continued to affect English art and artistic criticism.

In the case of Ruskin, the turning-point came in 1845 when, at the age of twenty-six, his adoring parents at last allowed him to go abroad alone. Whilst deeply moved by his discovery of the Italian Primitives, whose beauty he revealed to the world, it was however Jacopo della Quercia's monument at Lucca, where Ilaria di Caretto 'lies at rest like a fallen flower', which first impressed on him the full spiritual splendour of Christian art. That would be the beginning of his passionate love for the Quattrocento, which took him back to Venice and Verona again and again. Some of his most memorable writing was the fruit of his intensive studies of Italian Romanesque and Gothic.

Ruskin's artistic ideas and sense of beauty were thus nurtured by Italy, and it was there that 'his spirit burned most brightly'. If, moreover, he had never lived in Italy and experienced Italian light, he might never have developed the intense enthusiasm for vivid colour which he shared with the Pre-Raphaelites. Nor would he have been able to understand so well the splendid extravagances of Turner, whom he acclaimed as the supreme artist of his time. Ruskin's own description of an Italian scene in his *Modern Painters* shows how he could feel a similar emotional reaction to the colour and luminosity of the Mediterranean: 'I cannot call it colour, it was conflagration. Purple,

and crimson and scarlet, like the curtains of God's tabernacle . . .
quivering with buoyant and burning life.'

Although he was such an immensely influential figure in Victorian
England, Ruskin is little more than a name to most people now. Today,
when seers and preachers are out of fashion, he is apt to seem a tedious
and fallible prophet, his artistic prejudices wrong-headed and his
moralizing misplaced. But it would be difficult to deny the exceptional
perceptiveness of his vision; and his theories, which he knew how to
express in such poetic and persuasive prose, had an enormous impact
on Victorian taste, not least by opening English eyes to the neglected
glories of early Italian art. Ruskin's high-minded blend of aesthetics,
morality and sentiment was perfectly attuned to the new middle-class
public eager to be taught how to get the most out of their foreign
excursions; and his *Stones of Venice*, praising Italian Gothic at the
expense of what he called the 'pestilential' art of the Renaissance,
became the bible of many tourists of his generation who followed in
his footsteps to Italy.

Generally speaking, however, it would probably have been not so
much his travels as his school-days that were likely to have given the
average Victorian of the educated classes his deepest impressions of the
civilizations of the Mediterranean. Seeing, as they did, ancient Greece
through a golden haze, the Victorians were sometimes tempted to
picture themselves as the Greeks of the modern world, Spartan in
their public school training and Periclean in their combination of
imperialism with democracy and liberty. This was pre-eminently a
century of classical scholarship, when the encroachment of the sciences
had not yet deprived the classics of their traditional primacy in
education.

But in spite of all their compulsory Greek and Latin, the public
schools were in fact no less insular than the Victorians themselves.
The Mediterranean heritage could still arouse nostalgia, but it now
no longer bore such a vital meaning for the British who, like other
northern peoples, are by temperament more romantic than classical.
In so far as they allowed themselves to be distracted from their
preoccupation with the practical problems of their own times, the

Victorians were as a rule drawn to the Middle Ages rather than to Greek or Roman classicism: their prophets were Ruskin and Carlyle; their architecture Gothic. The stimulus to rescue British art and literature from mediocrity was eventually to come from France and Ireland, and not from Italy which had by this time ceased to be central to our culture.

CHAPTER 9

IN THE PRESENT
DECLENSION

In the Mediterranean lies the hope of humanity.
Norman Douglas, *South Wind*

The decline in the old Greek and Italian influences, which had already
set in before the end of the Victorian era, has accelerated in our own;
and now the Mediterranean heritage which the English had once so
highly prized has become more and more devalued. It could hardly
have remained unscathed amidst the tremendous upheavals of the
twentieth century which were loosening so many of our traditional
links with times gone by. The modern scientific and technological
revolution has been absorbing the best of our aspirations and the best
minds. When it was as much as they could do to try and keep abreast
of the bewildering new problems of a world that was being transformed
before their very eyes, few people any longer had either time or
inclination to concern themselves particularly with what may have
happened in a small group of Greek communities more than two
thousand years ago, or even with Renaissance Italy. Englishmen might
still retain a measure of sentimental nostalgia for this illustrious past,
but they found it increasingly difficult to believe that it could have
any vital relevance for them today.

As with so much else in modern history, the watershed was the
First World War, whose shattering impact swept away the old order

of things in Europe. In the early 1900s, virtually the only challenge
to the traditional values came from a small *avant-garde* minority, whose
ideas admittedly contained a startling preview of the revolutionary
changes that were to come. The English had not yet, for instance, lost
the general familiarity with the classics which made it seem quite
natural for politicians to use Greek and Latin quotations in their
speeches. Every educated man was assumed to have at least a grounding
in the ancient languages. Classical scholarship was still contributing to
the formation of literary taste and, apart from a handful of brilliant
exceptions, artists generally continued to conform to the humanistic
conventions inherited from the Italian Renaissance. For their part,
British educationalists remained faithful to their cherished belief that
for any member of the ruling political and intellectual classes, character
was more important than learning, and that this could best be inculcated by the disciplines of the classics. As Oscar Wilde put it,
in the mouth of one of his characters, 'examinations are of no value
whatsoever; if a man is a gentleman he knows quite enough, and if he
is not a gentleman, whatever he knows is bad for him.'

The classics still have their impassioned champions even today, and
it is not so very long ago that Compton Mackenzie, for example, went
so far as to assert that the decline of compulsory Latin and Greek had
cost us the British Empire. But they have been fighting a losing battle.
Under the growing pressure from new subjects which seemed of
greater practical utility in a more competitive civilization where the
emphasis was shifting to the sciences, our educational system has been
gradually relinquishing the classical ground on which it once so firmly
stood. The ancient world is still accepted to be a legitimate subject of
academic study for the experts, and in some respects we now know a
good deal more about it than we ever did before. But for the common
man, to whom we have been told this century properly belongs, the
humanities are considered to be merely a superfluous ornament. The
new educational objective is to produce vocationally trained specialists,
instead of gentlemanly amateurs.

This is only one aspect of the modern retreat from humanistic values
which has been both a cause and an effect of the eclipse of the old

Greek and Italian influences; others will be mentioned later in this chapter. It has made remarkably little difference that far more English people have been finding their way to Greece and Italy than ever in the past, now that foreign travel has become part of the way of life of the affluent society. The hordes of sun-worshippers who flock to the glossy playgrounds around the Mediterranean for a few brief weeks each summer go in a very different spirit to earlier travellers; and the jet-propelled package-tour is obviously poles apart from the Grand Tour that used to take our ancestors to Italy for years at a time and fired them with the ambition to infuse English society with a knowledge and love of the culture of the South. Gone is the old sense of wonder and discovery. Not culture but sun-tan has become the status-symbol which the average tourist wants to have to show for his Mediterranean exposure when he gets back home.

There are of course always exceptions to prove any rule. Naturally, by no means all the present generation of tourists have been entirely insensitive to their surroundings, 'missing so much and so much'. A modicum of sight-seeing continues to figure amongst the tourist attractions, and there are now even a number of package-tours which are specifically cultural in content. The spate of books devoted to the Greek and Italian cultural achievement has shown no signs of abating and seems to indicate that the subject retains its fascination for at any rate a minority of Englishmen, and particularly perhaps for those who have tasted classical culture by visiting our Stately Homes. For many people, the Mediterranean countries still remain the Promised Land.

Some English authors continue to find the Mediterranean world as stimulating a source of inspiration as ever. One writer with a particularly deep attachment to Italy was Osbert Sitwell, who was proud to claim that he belonged to Italy, to the Italian past and 'to that old and famous combination of Italian influence and English blood'. His and his brother's enthusiastic rhapsodies in praise of the South helped to reopen English eyes to the extraordinary diversity of natural and artistic beauty that Italy has to offer; and a similar service has been performed for Greece, since that country came into fashion, by Patrick Leigh Fermor and a host of other British writers.

It has no doubt remained as true as ever before that for a certain type of artistic genius contacts with Greece or Italy and their ancient civilizations can prove an experience of the greatest possible significance. E. M. Forster, two of whose novels have an Italian setting, is a case in point. His youthful imagination was captivated by the Mediterranean. If Greece seemed to him to stand for truth, Italy (where he lived for a time) stood for passion.

There is yet another respect in which English literature's debt to the southern world has continued to accumulate. It is usually the exceptionally sensitive and gifted artists who are most liable to pay the price of genius by feeling misfits, at odds with the constraints of the society of their own country. Sometimes this leads them to seek a haven abroad, where they can hope not only to find fresh sources of inspiration but, more important still, to regain the peace of spirit which they need so desperately in order to fulfil their genius. For two of the most famous writers of our times, James Joyce and D. H. Lawrence, the Mediterranean South provided this happy sense of liberation, as it had already done for Shelley and Byron and other 'outsiders' in the past.

But expatriation can seldom prove an easy undertaking, even when it is self-imposed. Although it soon became clear to Joyce that he would be obliged to leave Ireland in order to avoid being stifled by its narrow Catholicism, he never ceased to pine for his beloved Dublin, the half-mythical city of his memories and dreams which continued to obsess him and to be the constant subject of his writing. This reluctant exile spent over a decade between Pola, Trieste and Rome. It was an intensely unhappy period for Joyce, and he had little use for the South 'with its damn silly sun that turns men to butter'. None the less, in his freer surroundings his genius matured, and by the time he left Trieste in 1915 *Dubliners* had been published, *A Portrait of the Artist as a Young Man* completed, and a start had been made on his *magnum opus*. 'In Rome,' he was to write some years later, 'when I had finished about half the *Portrait*, I realized that the Odyssey had to be the sequel, and I began to write *Ulysses*.'

Italy was also the first place of exile for D. H. Lawrence after he had decided that he must escape from England and the soul-destroying values of materialist civilization to which his whole creed was so utterly opposed. He was as impatient as Joyce with the Italians when they failed to come up to his expectations, and he once caustically described Italy as 'man-gripped and withered . . . so tender – like cooked macaroni – yards and yards of soft tenderness ravelled round everything'.

But any new country always acted as a stimulus to Lawrence; and he liked to feel that in the more primitive parts of Italy there still survived an older, better way of life, more congenial to his own particular ideas. Besides his two novels, *The Lost Girl* and *Aaron's Rod*, his Mediterranean journeyings helped to inspire many of his poems and his travel books, including *Etruscan Places* which gave him the opportunity to depict an ideal society, fashioned less after history than after his own heart. Although he always remained a restless wanderer, his Odyssey in search of fulfilment brought Lawrence back to Italy in the end. It was then, whilst he was living at a farmhouse near Florence, that he wrote *Lady Chatterley's Lover*, and an echo of the soft Tuscan countryside can be detected in its gentle sensuality.

But the author who was able to achieve the most intimate understanding of Italy and the Mediterranean spirit was probably Norman Douglas, the Austrian-born Scot who had befriended Lawrence when he escaped from England after the First World War and arrived practically penniless in Florence. Douglas spent many years in Italy, getting to know and love this 'siren land' in a way few foreigners had ever done before, and writing of the country and its people with extraordinary perceptiveness and erudition. His *Old Calabria* ranks particularly high amongst the literature of travel. The island of Capri has inspired innumerable writers, but no book breathes its enchanted atmosphere better than *South Wind*, where Norman Douglas uses the brilliant talk as a vehicle for expounding his humanistic philosophy with all the limpid clarity of the pagan South; and he liked to imagine that the day would come when men would reject contemporary materialism and settle round the shores of the Mediterranean where they could lead serener lives.

Another Scottish author to find inspiration in his life-long love of the ancient classical world is Compton Mackenzie. He always felt a passion for islands, and Capri provided the setting for his two witty extravaganzas, *Vestal Fire* and *Extraordinary Women*. But with Compton Mackenzie, however, we come to a more modern generation for whom the magic of Greece and the Aegean often had greater significance than anything that Italy could offer. The latter has been paying the price for having become too familiar, whereas Greece has been more successful in retaining her less sophisticated and individual flavour. Even the stark beauty of the numinous Aegean landscape and the uncompromising clarity of the diamond-hard light seem better calculated to appeal to the present-day taste than do the softer contours of the Italian countryside.

Nowadays most of us are eager to swell the ranks of the philhellenes, and the new fashion for the reassuringly man-sized world of Greece has shaken the old pre-eminence of Italy for the artists and the writers, the dons and the romantic travellers. But the Italians, who were in any case never particularly flattered when foreigners insisted on treating their country as little more than a huge museum, have been discovering fresh ways in which to make their mark on the world. In our modern industrialized civilization, the same Italian genius for revolutionary innovation which in less scientific times used to find its expression mainly in the fine arts, now impresses us with achievements in engineering and film-making, for instance, and the mass-produced good taste of Italian designs for such things as motor-cars, clothes and jewellery. These have often managed to combine a trend-setting modernity with an element of artistic elegance which is especially valuable at a time when mediocrity has been threatening to become the general rule. We should be grateful, too, for the espresso bars and the restaurants, Greek and Cypriot as well as Italian, which have emerged as such a familiar feature of the English scene, helping to civilize our cooking.

But whatever Italy's many contributions to the amenities of modern life and despite the popular discovery of the enchantment of Greece, we have obviously come a very long way indeed from the days when these ancient lands enjoyed a privileged position in the eyes of successive generations of Englishmen who regarded them, sometimes with almost mystical awe, as the sacred fountainhead of their own civilization. It is not only that in the scientific world of today less place seems to have been left for the spiritual and cultural values which we used to treasure. The ancient classical culture has lost the unique qualities it once had for us, and we now hesitate to assume that it enjoyed any monopoly of wisdom. In the present century our European continent has been shorn of its age-old supremacy, not only in politics and commerce, but over the very minds of the Europeans themselves. With the modern revolution in communications came an enormous expansion of our intellectual and artistic horizons. We have been made aware of other civilizations, whose cultural traditions are very different but not necessarily inferior to our own.

We have burst out of the confines of our old European culture. To many young people nowadays, some watered-down mysticism derived from Asian philosophy seems far more exciting than anything they can discover in the classics. New art forms are constantly being borrowed from outside Europe. The modern composer has often felt the fascination of oriental music; and the popular enthusiasm aroused by the negro jazz musicians is common knowledge. The unfamiliar and exotic have grown to be the fashion, so that artists have frequently found some primitive African carving more moving than classical Greek sculpture, for example; whilst if they want to work abroad, they now tend to go as far afield as, say, Mexico or California, instead of taking the well-worn path to Tuscany and Rome. . . . For a multitude of reasons, therefore, English interest in the Mediterranean civilizations has been on the wane – even though we cannot help still sometimes envying their easier way of life, and would dearly love to learn the secret of this long tradition of the 'dolce vita'.

There is one respect, however, in which the ancient classical world has acquired a fresh significance for the modern mind. This is as the result of the enhanced significance now once again attached to *myth*. Classical mythology, with its treasure-hoard of story, has been part of the common heritage of Europe since time immemorial. Each generation could find its own message in these perennial daydreams of the human spirit which have haunted men's imagination through the ages. Certain immortal themes from Greek mythology, like the search of Ulysses, the maze and the Minotaur, and the descent to the Underworld, possess an apparently unending fertility, constantly provoking fresh interpretations and ideas. They have served as an inexhaustible source of inspiration to the poets, who are themselves weavers of myth after their own fashion and have used them to awaken the sleeping poetry in our souls.

Renewed interest in the ancient myths was first stimulated by writers like Frazer and Max Müller in the last century. Once they had been reinterpreted by Freud and his successors, they could no longer be dismissed as merely picturesque old stories, but came to be regarded as revealing eternal verities containing a vital message for modern man which can help him to a deeper understanding of his own nature. Appealing simultaneously to our emotions, our intelligence and our imagination, they have recaptured the contemporary mind as much thanks to the clues they appear to provide to the solution of our human problems, as though their poetry which so often startles us into heightened awareness.

Freud's own speculations sometimes seem more akin to poetry than science, as he himself may have recognized when he said, 'not I, but the poets discovered the unconscious'. They reinforced the theory, already launched by the Symbolists, that the magical speech of the poets should, like the magic language of myth, above all consist of symbols. To many of the latter Freud ascribed a new and more sinister meaning. But still more far-reaching implications were attributed to the myths by Freud's pupil, Jung. He believed them to be embodiments of what he called the 'collective unconscious', in which were accumulated the age-old memories of the human race, with all its ceaseless longings and frustrations. He saw them as the timeless expression of archetypal imagery fundamental to man's psyche. This great thinker has made us realize how closely mythology, religion and poetry are interwoven, each being concerned in its own way to come to terms with the blind forces of nature within and without us.

Even in this coldly scientific age, when Christianity itself sometimes tends to be reduced to just another, if exceptionally powerful, system of mythology, the instinctive human need for myth persists as strongly as ever. At one level this expresses itself in people's appetite for the debased myths of advertisement and propaganda. But there is much more to it than that. For although many of the new theories were highly abstruse and controversial, the basic ideas involved have gained a remarkably wide measure of public acceptance. They colour the popular outlook on the whole present-day world, and even schoolboys who no longer get a classical education can talk glibly of the complex of Oedipus. Literature has seized on the deeper meanings now attributed to myth, using them to help its explorations of the frontiers of experience and to illuminate the dark corners of the human mind. Both in England and abroad, the Greek legends have stirred the imagination of numerous contemporary writers, and they have retold the old stories in a more modern idiom, often giving a new twist to their significance.

James Joyce's *Ulysses* provides an example of the fresh uses which the modern artist has found for the ancient legends, and it becomes easier to decipher the riddles of this extremely important but very complex book, as also of Joyce's *Finnegans Wake*, if the author's Greek sources of inspiration are taken into account. Ulysses was always Joyce's favourite hero ever since he first read about him in Charles Lamb at the age of twelve. He had a fellow-feeling for this wanderer who, like himself, was possessed with a passionate love for his native country but condemned to a long exile far from home.

It is therefore not surprising that the story of the *Odyssey* should have occurred to Joyce when he came to compose his masterpiece. Transposed in time and place to cover a day in the lives of a group of Dubliners, it served him as a framework for the vast variety of experiences which he wanted to include in his own epic. He began by borrowing from Homer many of his characters and even more of his situations. Most of these props were progressively discarded as he went along, and the Homeric design ultimately became overlaid with so many other interlocking motifs that it is often almost unrecognizable, turning into a parody of the heroics of the original. But there can be little question that without his use of Homeric parallels it would have been far more difficult for Joyce to transform his obscure Dublin characters into memorable symbols of the tragi-comedy of human existence.

In a review of *Ulysses* published in 1923 T. S. Eliot, whose revolutionary influence on the development of modern poetry may be compared with that of Joyce on modern prose, applauded Joyce's use of myth 'as a way of controlling or ordering, of giving a shape and a significance to the immense panorama of futility and anarchy which is contemporary history'. Eliot employed a rather similar method himself, making constant use of metaphor and myth in order to give a deeper dimension to the surface realities of present-day life by relating them to a different, more primitive kind of experience. By means of an intricate pattern of recondite allusions, many of them taken from mythology or the classics, he was able to create a timeless world, where golf captains became identified with captains of Roman legions, and 'Madame Sosostris, famous clairvoyante' was, as it were, the reincarnation of the ancient Greek seer Tiresias, whom his notes on *The Waste Land* call 'the most important personage in the poem'. Intensely concerned with the spiritual plight of modern man, Eliot drew from the old legends images to illustrate humanity's yearning for regeneration, and he threw the evils of twentieth-century materialism into sharper relief by superimposing on its squalors the loveliness of classical art and myth.

His 'Sweeney Among the Nightingales' provides a particularly arresting illustration of his technique. Eliot caustically describes a brutish contemporary tavern scene. But he suddenly breaks off and brings the poem to a close on a very different note, evocative of the majesty of Greek tragedy,

> The nightingales are singing near
> The Convent of the Sacred Heart,
> And sang within the bloody wood
> When Agamemnon cried aloud,
> And let their liquid siftings fall
> To stain the stiff dishonoured shroud.

Such irony fulfils a dual purpose. It can hardly fail to shock the reader into heightened attention; and by the counterpoint created through this deliberate play on contrasting levels of meaning and experience, Eliot skilfully deepens both the emotional impact and the human implications of his poetry.

Eliot was emphatically a modernist. But in common with his friend Ezra Pound, 'il miglior fabbro', to whom he dedicated *The Waste Land*, he had a profound conviction of the relevance of the classics to contemporary literature. He believed that the old cultures must provide the elements to fertilize the new. For a long time he was preoccupied with the legend of Oedipus and with Aeschylus' *Oresteia*, finding inspiration in the *Eumenides* for his play *The Family Reunion*. He aimed to translate past literary values into his own modernistic poetry. Eager to see the classics transposed into a living contemporary idiom, he objected to the 'vulgar debasement' of Gilbert Murray's renderings of Greek poetry in the flaccid style of Swinburne, because he felt that this deprived it of its power to revitalize our own. Convinced that 'modern scholarship about the past could illuminate the darkness of the present', he appealed for a careful study of the Renaissance humanists and translators. He was insistent that the modern poet must develop a consciousness of the past, even though that might involve the 'continual extinction of his personality'. What we need, he urged, is 'an eye which can see the past in its place with its definite differences from the present, and yet so lively that it shall be as present to us as the present'. That was his definition of the 'creative eye'.

Eliot was not an outstanding linguist and disclaimed any specialist knowledge of Greek or Latin. Whatever he lacked in expert scholarship, however, he made up for in his enthusiasm, and at one time he became president both of the Classical Association and of the Virgil Society. Similarly, his Italian was only sketchy, but he endeavoured to teach himself enough of the language to enable him to read Dante in the original. This was the poet whom Eliot acknowledged to have had 'the most persistent and deepest influence' on his verse, although he may in fact, as F. R. Leavis has argued, have overvalued what Dante could offer him in relation to his own particular quest. He frequently borrowed images from the *Divine Comedy*, and he dedicated a short monograph to its author, where he argues that the modern poet has more to learn from Dante than from any more recent writer. Being himself so concerned with the two great traditions of Western civilization, the Christian and the classical, he recognized in Dante a kindred spirit for whose philosophy he came to feel an increasing reverence. He placed him even higher than Shakespeare because, he said, his poetry seemed to illustrate 'a saner attitude towards the mystery of life'.

If T. S. Eliot deserves such a relatively large place in this survey, it is because he was the last of the major English poets to possess a passionate faith in the living value of tradition, lending his great authority to the championship of the Mediterranean heritage as intensely relevant to modern art. This American who adopted Europe so whole-heartedly had a deep sense of history and of cultural continuity. Although he developed a vision and technique that were individual and new, he remained wedded to the traditional values, showing how an acute feeling for the past need not be an obstacle to revolutionary innovation but can, on the contrary, actually be made to contribute to it. It was not, he insisted, that the new way of writing was destructive of the past or repudiated it, 'but that we have enlarged our conception of the past; and that in the light of what is new we see the past in a new pattern'.

It might have been supposed that Eliot's example would have conclusively demonstrated to the modernists that it was by no means essential to turn their backs on the past in order to achieve the personal vision and technical novelty to which they attached such overriding importance. This lesson seems to have been largely lost on them, however, at least in so far as the *avant-garde* is concerned. Even D. H. Lawrence derided Eliot's antiquarian 'classiosity' as 'bunkum'; and although the 'revolutionary traditionalism' of Pound and Eliot set a standard for the poets down until the last war, now poetry has moved on again under the impact of an American reaction against the European traditionalism of the previous generation. Eliot's intricate classical allusions can, in any case, hardly be expected to retain much meaning for a public that no longer possesses the same cultural background as poets were able to take for granted in the time of Milton or Tennyson or even Eliot's own. Now that nearly every reference has to be elaborately explained in a footnote, the gentle art of allusion has lost its erstwhile magic.

Eliot's exceptional sense of commitment to traditional values would therefore be almost inconceivable in any young writer of today. But his frequent use of metaphor and myth is, on the other hand, by no means uncommon amongst more recent authors, and particularly amongst those poets who have continued to write in the Romantic tradition, raising their voices in protest against the spiritual barrenness of the age. Like poets from time immemorial, the modern poets have drawn not only on their own world of dreams but have sought to enlarge the significance of their poetry by drawing on the dreams of bygone generations as well, feeding their imagination on the sacred mysteries of the mythical past.

One of those who knew how to use myth to considerable effect was Edith Sitwell, especially in her maturer work where the blending of classical and Christian sometimes produces great lyrical vitality. For some poets, the new psycho-analytical interpretations of the myths have assumed a particular significance, and archetypal imagery has frequently been employed by George Barker, Roy Fuller and Kathleen Raine, amongst others. An obsession with mythology also emerges very clearly from the writings of Robert Graves, who is steeped in ancient Mediterranean lore and has a profound feeling for the southern world where he has made his home.

Even Yeats had a life-long love of classical poetry and myth which was never completely eclipsed by his deeper fascination with the twilight Celtic past; and his belief in the 'Great Memory', the memory of Nature herself, seems to have brought him close to Jung's ideas of the 'collective unconscious'. He weaves the magic of Greece and his own neo-Platonism into many of his poems, and in one of his later volumes, *The Tower*, he concludes, after invoking Plato and Plotinus, Helen and Homer,

> I have prepared my peace
> With learned Italian things
> And the proud stones of Greece. . . .

But Yeats was writing for an earlier age, when the Grecian Urn had not yet cracked. Now, there are very different poetic trends, either towards the esoteric and hermetic or towards histrionic declamation.

Contemporary artists have often been no less responsive than the poets to the suggestiveness of myth. But the modern artistic revolution has progressively submerged nearly all of their other links with the Mediterranean past. British art had hitherto almost always remained basically humanistic, even in the Romantic age when there was a reaction against a classical style which had degenerated into the stereotyped repetition and ornamentation of classicism. Mediterranean traditions provided countless generations of artists with a coherent scaffolding on which to build. In our own times, however, these well-tried sources of inspiration have become discredited. The modern artist has generally been so preoccupied with the cult of revolutionary novelty that such relics of the past seem to him to have lost their deeper relevance.

Thus, in these days there are only comparatively few painters, sculptors or architects who still find the best nourishment of their genius in what Graham Sutherland has called 'the continual rediscovery of the past', and even fewer who would have the courage to make such an unfashionable admission if they did. Sutherland himself belongs to this dwindling minority. So, in many respects, does Henry Moore, who studied in Italy and now often works there at his house near the Carrara mountains.

Moore is universally admired as the first sculptor of undisputed genius that this usually unsculptural nation has ever managed to produce, and part of the secret of his pre-eminence may be that he is too great an individualist to have felt it necessary to conform to the popular prejudice which now inhibits so many lesser artists from accepting inspiration from the past. He has, on the contrary, always been ready to emphasize how much he owes to earlier artists, and not least to the Renaissance masters such as Masaccio and Michelangelo.

It is difficult to understand him unless we realize that the latter has always been his special hero, whom he reveres as the supreme sculptor of all time. And he has praised Giovanni Pisano, the last and greatest of the medieval classicists, in terms which proclaim the essential humanism of his own artistic ideals. 'I feel terribly strongly', he wrote not very long ago, 'that he was a great man because he understood human beings and if you asked me how I would judge great artists it would be on this basis.' In Pisano, he said, 'the human and the abstract formal elements were inseparable and that is what I think really great sculpture should be.'

Kenneth Clark has pointed out in his brilliant study on the nude that Moore, whilst searching for new forms, 'yet gives to his constructions the same fundamental character which was invented by the sculptors of the Parthenon in the fifth century before Christ'. Like his fellow sculptor Barbara Hepworth, he stands in fact much nearer to the humanistic Mediterranean tradition than the great majority of present-day artists. The basically classical nature of his approach is apparent in his concentration on general conceptions with a universal implication, such as 'the mother and child', in preference to more particularized subjects. Even in its most revolutionary abstractions his sculpture retains an element of classical serenity and a profound feeling for the human form.

It must be recognized, however, that Henry Moore by this time represents an outstanding exception in what has become an essentially unclassical age. No less than Joyce and Eliot, he properly belongs to the first great phase of the modern artistic revolution, which rejected academism but did not altogether break with the past. The Renaissance criterion of the 'human scale' was not entirely jettisoned at first, even by the abstract painters and sculptors, and the Greek-derived convention of the nude survived to link the arts with their Mediterranean heritage. Although so many of the established canons were already being challenged, it was still generally accepted that great art ought to possess certain positive, life-enhancing qualities, through which it could give a fresh dimension and deeper meaning to our lives. Even those artists and writers who were most eagerly searching after new gods often continued to cast back nostalgic glances at the lost classical culture.

But since then the anti-traditionalist reaction has been pushed to increasingly violent extremes, and the human figure, for example, no longer retains the same artistic primacy as it had almost continuously enjoyed since the days of ancient Greece. There is a growing tendency to dismiss the most time-honoured principles as outworn clichés, and even to question whether art needs any rules at all in this permissive age. We have seen how the Mediterranean traditions had already been losing their power of providing a living source of inspiration. By now, however, the latest wave of the artistic revolution is threatening to sweep away the little that is still left of them, including what was perhaps the most important tradition of them all – the natural community of understanding between the artist and his public.

Nowadays, few artists regard the legacy of the past as a priceless quarry where they can discover elements for new creation; they generally see it rather as an oppressive burden from which they must shake themselves free. In this twilight of the old culture, 'the tyranny of tradition' has become a favourite slogan with the *avant-garde*. Such a disparaging expression would have been almost inconceivable at any earlier period. But it epitomizes the disenchantment of a generation which feels that it has at last outgrown the well-ordered, too familiar world of Greece and Rome.

It is, indeed, perfectly possible that today's iconoclasts will be proved right. The Mediterranean heritage has had a very long innings and may by this time have little more to give us. It certainly seems hardly likely ever to reassume anything approaching its former significance for the English, and it may be that we have come to the end of this long story.

And yet it is difficult to believe that the creative impulse of classicism must be finally relegated to the museum. It has shaped our culture from the start. Nor can it be purely fortuitous that the great high-water marks of British civilization so often coincided with the times when we were most susceptible to the Mediterranean enchantment, during the Elizabethan Renaissance, for instance, and again in the eighteenth century and the Romantic age. Even today, its forms and principles are present, intricately woven into much of the art of our time, though temporarily unacknowledged and obscured.

However worn the old coinage has become, and however anxious the English may now be to repudiate so much of their past, they can hardly deny their Mediterranean heritage. Ever since the Roman occupation nearly two thousand years ago, it has been contributing to their civilization, helping them to mould their institutions and values, and their whole thinking. I like to believe that it will remain a living force.

> Though the great song return no more
> There's keen delight in what we have –
> A rattle of pebbles on the shore
> Under the receding wave.
>
> W. B. Yeats

BIBLIOGRAPHY

Apart from the essential authorities mentioned in the body of the text, there are, of course, an enormous variety of more recent books bearing on different aspects of the subject.

Gilbert Highet's *The Classical Tradition* (Oxford University Press, 1949) provides an excellent introduction to the history of the classical influences on European literature, which I found extremely helpful in clarifying my own ideas. I am also greatly indebted to Kenneth Clark's brilliantly perceptive writings on English and Italian art. I have repeatedly drawn on his *Landscape into Art* (John Murray, 1949) in order to illustrate the British landscape painters' response to Italian inspiration; and I was unable to resist the temptation to borrow his title and reverse it in order to make a chapter-heading of my own.

The following can also be particularly recommended:

Cultural History of England, F. Halliday, Thames & Hudson, 1967.
The Beginnings of English Society, D. Whitelock, Penguin, 1952.
The Flowering of the Middle Ages, ed. J. Evans, Thames & Hudson, 1966.
The Great Pilgrimage of the Middle Ages, V. and H. Hell, Barrie & Rockliff, 1966.
The Age of the Renaissance, ed. D. Hay, Thames & Hudson, 1967.
Sir Philip Sidney and the English Renaissance, J. Buxton, Macmillan, 1964.
John Milton, Englishman, J. Hanford, Gollancz, 1950.
Grand Tour, ed. R. Lambert, Faber & Faber, 1935.
The Grand Tour, C. Hibbert, Weidenfeld & Nicolson, 1969.

Four Portraits, P. Quennell, Collins, 1945.

The Rule of Taste, J. Steegman, Macmillan, 1968.

Earls of Creation, J. Lees-Milne, Hamish Hamilton, 1962.

The Georgians at Home, E. Burton, Longmans, Green, 1967.

British Art and the Mediterranean, F. Saxl and R. Wittkower, Oxford University Press, 1948.

British Architecture and its Background, J. Nellist, Macmillan, 1967.

The Englishness of English Art, N. Pevsner, Architectural Press, 1956.

British Architects and Craftsmen, S. Sitwell, Batsford, 1945.

Palladio and English Palladianism, R. Wittkower, Thames & Hudson, 1974.

The English House through Seven Centuries, O. Cook, Nelson, 1968.

English Neo-Classical Art, D. Irwin, Faber & Faber, 1966.

Italian Landscape in Eighteenth-Century England, E. Mainwaring, Cass, 1965.

The Picturesque, C. Hussey, Putnam, 1927.

English Gardens and Landscapes, 1700–1750, C. Hussey, Country Life, 1967.

Sculpture in Britain, 1530–1830, M. Whinney, Penguin, 1964.

A History of British Music, P. Young, Benn, 1967.

Italy and the English Romantics, C. Brand, Cambridge University Press, 1957.

The Italian Influence in English Poetry, L. Sells, Allen & Unwin, 1955.

English Bards and Greek Marbles, S. Larrabee, New York, 1943.

Shelley, S. Spender, Longmans, Green, 1952.

Keats and the Mirror of Art, I. Jack, Oxford University Press, 1967.

Mythology and the Romantic Tradition in English Poetry, D. Bush, Harvard University Press, 1937.

The Golden Ring, G. Treves, Longmans, Green, 1956.

James Joyce, H. Gorman, Bodley Head, 1941.

The Sacred Wood, T. S. Eliot, Methuen, 1920.

Dante, T. S. Eliot, Faber & Faber, 1929.

Mirror of Minds, G. Bullough, Athlone Press, 1962.

British Art since 1900, J. Rothenstein, Phaidon Press, 1962.

The Italians, L. Barzini, Hamish Hamilton, 1964.

NAME INDEX

Adam, Robert, 67, 73–7, 81, 117
Addison, Joseph, 47–8, 56, 112
Aeschylus, 130, 161
Albania, 134
Alcuin, 12
Aldhelm, St, 12, 18
Alfieri, Vittorio, 136
Alfred the Great, 13, 18
Ali Pasha, 134
Anselm, St, 14
Aretino, Pietro, 26
Ariosto, Ludovico, 31, 124
Aristotle, 18, 22
Arnold, Matthew, 143, 146
Athens, 134; see also Parthenon
Augustine, St, 8
Austen, Jane, 115

Bacon, Francis, 26, 27
Baedeker, Karl, 142
Baker, Sir Herbert, 84
Balfe, Michael, 147
Bank of England, 81
Bari, 16
Barker, George, 163
Barry, Charles, 82, 83
Bath, 72

Beckford, Peter, 49
Bede, Venerable, 11, 12, 18
Bennett, Arnold, 145
Bernini, Giovanni Lorenzo, 66, 89
Bishop, Sir Henry, 147
Blake, William, 77, 93, 125
Blenheim Palace, 67
Boccaccio, Giovanni, 23, 124, 146
Boethius, 13
Bologna, 18
Boniface, St, 12
Bonington, Richard Parkes, 99
Boswell, James, 49, 57
Botticelli, Sandro, 49
Brawne, Fanny, 130
Bridgeman, Charles, 115
Brougham, Henry Peter, Lord, 56
Brown, Lancelot ('Capability'), 117–18
Browning, Elizabeth Barrett, 141, 144–5
Browning, Robert, 141, 144–5
Bruno, Giordano, 132
Buckingham Palace, 114
Burlington, Lord, 53, 54, 56, 67, 68–71,
    72, 91, 115
Burney, Dr Charles, 55
Burton, Decimus, 80
Burton, Robert, 42

Byrd, William, 38, 39
Byron, George Gordon, Lord, 50, 123, 125, 126, 133–7, 139, 140

Caboto, Giovanni (John Cabot), 22
Calabria, 14
Cambridge, 18
Cameron, Charles, 76
Campbell, Colen, 69
Canaletto, Antonio, 51, 96–7
Canova, Antonio, 76, 80
Canterbury, 14, 16
Carlton House, 80
Carracci, Annibale, 95
Carrara, 164
Casanova, Giovanni Jacopo, 49
Castiglione, Baldassare, 26, 27–8, 34
Castle Howard, 67
Cavour, Camillo, 141, 144
Cecil, Robert, 110
Cellini, Benvenuto, 49
Cerutti, Angelo, 145
Chambers, Sir William, 72, 78, 117, 118
Charlemagne, 12
Charles I, 40, 64, 88–9
Charles II, 46
Chaucer, Geoffrey, 15, 23–4, 31
Chelsea, 110
Chesterfield, Lord, 48
Chichester, 16
Chippendale, Thomas, 77
Chiswick House, 70, 116
Cipriani, 77
Clairmont, Allegra, 126
Clark, Kenneth, 102, 165
Claude Lorraine, 47, 60, 75, 97–8, 101, 102, 104, 107, 109, 112, 113, 115, 116, 117, 132
Coke, Thomas, Earl of Leicester, 71–2, 116
Coleridge, Samuel Taylor, 132–3
Coleshill House, 64
Colet, John, 24
Como, 133

Constable, John, 102, 104
Constantine, Emperor, 8
Constantinople, 22, 134
Cook, Olive, 68
Cook, Thomas, 142
Cooper, John, 38
Copernicus, Nicolaus, 43
Cornwall, 6
Corsica, 57
Cozens, J. R., 99

Dante Alighieri, 23, 24, 26, 30, 36, 37, 124, 128–9, 130, 136, 142, 146, 161–2
Danvers, John, 110
Defoe, Daniel, 52
Dickens, Charles, 59, 140, 145
Donatello, 49
Donne, John, 5, 43
Douglas, Norman, 151, 155
Dowland, John, 38
Drayton, Michael, 42
Dryden, John, 56, 67
Dublin, 154
Dunstan, St, 13
Durham, 16

Edinburgh, 81
Elgin, Lord, 80
Eliot, George, 145
Eliot, T. S., 32, 160–3
Elizabeth I, 24–5, 29, 40, 87
Elssler, Fanny, 147
Erasmus, Desiderius, 24
Etna, 50
Eton, 46
Evelyn, John, 51, 110

Fermor, Patrick Leigh, 153
Fishbourne, 7
Florence, 26, 36, 49–50, 95, 144–5, 155
Florio, John, 25
Fontainebleau, 110
Forster, E. M., 154

Frazer, Sir James, 158
Freud, Sigmund, 158
Fry, Roger, 83, 104
Fuller, Roy, 163

Gainsborough, Thomas, 94–5, 100–1
Galileo, 43
Garibaldi, Giuseppe, 141
Garrick, David, 49
Gaskell, Mrs Elizabeth, 145
Gay, John, 55
George I, 111
George III, 96
George IV, 117
Gibbon, Edward, 49, 56, 57–9, 124, 128
Gibbons, Grinling, 67
Gibbons, Orlando, 38
Gillray, James, 95
Gissing, George, 145
Gladstone, William Ewart, 142
Goldsmith, Oliver, 56
Graves, Robert, 163
Greenwich, 65, 66, 89
Gregory the Great, Pope, 8, 12
Gregory VII, Pope, 14
Greville, Fulke, 29
Guardi, Francesco, 49
Guiccioli, Teresa, 136

Hadrian (seventh-century missionary), 9
Hamilton, Gavin, 76, 100
Hamilton, Sir William, 50–1
Hampton Court, 89, 110
Handel, George Frederick, 54–5
Hare, Augustus, 142
Hatfield House, 110
Hawksmoor, Nicholas, 67, 68
Haydon, Benjamin, 80, 131, 132
Hazlitt, William, 124, 145
Hellespont, 134
Henry II, 14
Henry III, 15
Henry VII, 24, 25
Henry VIII, 19, 24, 62, 88

Hepworth, Barbara, 165
Herculaneum, 73, 76
Herodotus, 6
Hertford, Lady, 51, 94
Hervey, Frederick, Earl of Bristol, 59–60, 70
Hexham, 10
Highet, Gilbert, 128
Hilliard, Nicholas, 88
Hogarth, William, 90–1, 95, 106
Holbein, Hans, 88
Holkham Hall, 71–2
Holland, Henry, 80
Hollis, Thomas, 99
Homer, 22, 56, 130, 132, 133, 142, 159
Honorius, Emperor, 8
Horace, 37, 47, 50, 56
Hyde Park, 115
Hyde Park Corner, 80

India, 84

John of Salisbury, 14
Johnson, Dr Samuel, 1, 27, 45, 56, 57
Jones, Inigo, 54, 62–5, 67, 68, 69, 91
Jonson, Ben, 32, 41
Joyce, James, 154, 159–60
Jung, Carl, 158, 163

Kauffman, Angelica, 77
Keats, John, 80, 130–2, 139, 140
Kedelston Hall, 74, 117
Kensington Gardens, 113
Kent, William, 53, 67, 69–72, 77, 113, 115–17
Kew, 117
Kneller, Sir Godfrey, 88, 90

Lake District, 114–15
Landor, Walter Savage, 124, 145, 146
Lanfranc, Archbishop of Canterbury, 14
Lawrence, D. H., 154–5, 162
Lawrence, Sir Thomas, 94, 103
Layard, Sir Austen Henry, 145

Le Nôtre, André, 110, 118
Lear, Edward, 106
Leavis, F. R., 161
Leighton, Lord, 148
Lely, Sir Peter, 88
Leoni, Giacomo, 71
Leptis Magna, 117
Lerici, Gulf of, 130
Liverpool, Lord, 124
London, 7, 24, 64–6, 70, 80–3, 88–90,
 110, 113, 114, 115
Longhi, Pietro, 49
Louis XIV, 46, 67
Lucca, 144, 148
Lullingstone, 7
Lutyens, Sir Edwin, 84
Lytton, Bulwer, 145

Macaulay, Lord, 124, 145
Macbeth, 14
Machiavelli, Niccolò, 26–7
Mackenzie, Compton, 152, 156
Malory, Sir Thomas, 31
Malmesbury, 16
Mann, Sir Horace, 49–50
Mantua, 35
Marenzio, Luca de, 39
Marie-Antoinette, 118
Martial, 47
Medici, Lorenzo de', 38
Meredith, George, 145
Mereworth Castle, 69, 70
Michelangelo, 31, 49, 92, 93
Milton, John, 29, 32, 35–8, 43–4
Missolonghi, 137
Mont Cenis pass, 48
Montagu, Lady Mary Wortley, 51
Moore, Henry, 41, 164–5
Morley, Thomas, 39
Morris, William, 105
Müller, Max, 158
Murray, Gilbert, 161
Murray, John, 142

Naples, 50–1
Napoleon Bonaparte, 48
Nash, John, 72, 75, 81–2, 115
National Gallery, 80
New Delhi, 84
Newman, Cardinal, 143
North, Thomas, 32

Osterley Park, 74
Ovid, 32, 33, 131
Oxford, 18, 24, 92

Padua, 26, 29, 46
Paestum, 50
Palladio, Andrea, and Palladianism, 46,
 62, 63–6, 68, 69, 70–3, 75, 82, 84
Pallavicino, Sir Horatio, 25
Palmer, Samuel, 99
Palmerston, Lord, 83, 142
Paoli, General, 57
Paris, 66, 105
Parthenon, 80, 132, 134
Pater, Walter, 145
Paulinus (seventh-century missionary), 8
Pavlovsk, 76
Peel, Sir Robert, 124
Pellegrini, G. A., 89–90
Pepin the Short, 12
Petrarch, Francesco, 23, 24, 30–1, 36,
 129, 133
Pevsner, Sir Nikolaus, 62
Phidias, 80
Piazza di Spagna, Rome, 99, 148
Piranesi, G. B., 78
Pisa, 16
Pisano, Giovanni, 165
Plato, 22, 31, 130
Plutarch, 32
Pompeii, 50, 73, 76
Pope, Alexander, 56, 72, 85, 112
Pound, Ezra, 161, 162
Poussin, Nicolas, 47, 60, 97, 101, 104,
 113, 115, 131–2
Puccini, Giacomo, 147

Pugin, A. W. N., 82–3
Purcell, Henry, 54, 67

Quercia, Jacopo della, 148

Raeburn, Sir Henry, 94
Raine, Kathleen, 163
Raphael, 53, 74, 92, 105
Ravenna, 136
Repton, Humphry, 118, 119
Reynolds, Sir Joshua, 76, 91–5, 97, 98,
    103, 105, 107, 117
Richardson, Jonathan, 87
Ripon, 10
Romano, Giulio, 35, 131
Rome, 6–22, 50, 58–9, 63, 78, 91, 95,
    98, 99–100, 106, 116, 121, 123,
    127–8, 130, 145, 148, 154
Romney, George, 76, 93, 94
Rosa, Salvator, 101, 104, 113
Rossetti, Dante Gabriel, 49, 105
Rossini, Gioacchino, 147
Rousseau, Jean-Jacques, 114, 118
Rowlandson, Thomas, 95
Rubens, Peter Paul, 88, 89, 112
Ruskin, John, 49, 82, 99, 104, 142, 143,
    148–9, 150
Russell, Lord John, 124, 142
Ruthwell, 11

St-Denis, 17
St James's Park, 110
St Paul's Cathedral, 66–7
Salerno, 18
Scott, Sir George Gilbert, 83
Scott, Sir Walter, 125, 145
Seneca, 32, 34
Shaftesbury, Lord, 53, 112
Shakespeare, William, 2, 29, 31–5, 42,
    43
Shelley, Mary, 126, 127, 128
Shelley, Percy Bysshe, 121, 122, 125,
    126–30, 139, 140
Sicily, 14–15, 50

Sidney, Sir Philip, 28–30, 41
Siena, 50
Simplon pass, 48
Sitwell, Edith, 163
Sitwell, Sir Osbert, 153
Smirke, Sir Robert, 79, 80
Smith, Joseph, 51
Smollett, Tobias, 56–7
Soane, Sir John, 81
Somerset House, 72
Sounion, 134
Spalato, 73
Spenser, Edmund, 29–31, 42
Sterne, Laurence, 57
Stonehenge, 6
Stourhead Park, 116
Stowe, 115, 116
Strawberry Hill, 74
Surrey, Earl of, 30
Sutherland, Graham, 164
Syon House, 74

Taglioni, Marie, 147
Taine, Hippolyte, 106
Tasso, Torquato, 31, 124
Tennyson, Alfred, Lord, 146
Thackeray, William Makepeace, 82, 145
Theodore (seventh-century missionary), 9
Thomas à Becket, 19
Thornhill, Sir James, 67, 89–90
Tintoretto, 105
Titian, 92, 105, 112, 131
Torrigiano, Pietro, 24
Towne, Francis, 99
Trollope, Anthony, 145
Tsarskoe Selo, 76
Turin, 49
Turner, J. M. W., 99, 102–4, 106, 148
Twickenham, 112

Vallombrosa, 36
Van Dyck, Sir Anthony, 88–9, 94
Van Gogh, Vincent, 103
Vanbrugh, Sir John, 54, 67, 68

Venice and the Venetian school, 26, 29, 45–6, 49, 85, 88–9, 96–7, 99, 103, 126, 133, 135, 145, 148
Verdi, Giuseppe, 147
Verona, 148
Verrio, Antonio, 89
Versailles, 67, 110
Vespucci, Amerigo, 22
Vesuvius, 50, 99
Vicenza, 63
Victoria, Queen, 139, 144, 147
Vignola, 62
Vikings, 13
Villa Capra ('Rotonda'), 69
Virgil, 31, 47, 50, 56, 112
Vitruvius, 62
Viviani, Emilia, 129

Wagner, Richard, 147
Walpole, Sir Horace, 49–50, 59, 72, 74, 101, 113, 115, 118, 124
Walter of the Mill, Archbishop of Palermo, 14
Walton, Izaak, 46
Wedgwood, Josiah, 77
Wellington, Duke of, 109

West, Benjamin, 76
Westminster Abbey, 24
Whitehall Palace, 64, 88
Wilde, Oscar, 147, 152
Wilfrid, St, 12
Wilkins, William, 80
William the Conqueror, 13–14, 15
William of Orange, 67, 111
Wilson, Richard, 98–9
Winckelmann, Johann, 79
Windsor, 81, 89
Wolsey, Cardinal, 24
Wotton, Sir Henry, 46, 62
Wordsworth, William, 101, 114, 133
Wren, Christopher, 65–7, 69
Wright, Joseph, 99
Wyatt, Jeffry, 81
Wyatt, Sir Thomas, 30

Yeats, W. B., 163–4, 167
York, 10, 12, 70
Younge, Nicholas, 38

Zuccaro, Federigo, 40
Zucchi, 77

GENERAL INDEX

Aaron's Rod, 155
Anatomy of Melancholy, The, 42
'Ancient Mariner, The', 133
Antony and Cleopatra, 32
archaeology, 50–1, 73, 76, 77
As You Like It, 33
'Atalanta in Calydon', 146

Baroque, 66, 67, 77, 88, 89, 110
Beggar's Opera, The, 55
By the Ionian Sea, 145
Byzantine, 15, 16

Canterbury Tales, The, 23
caricature, 95
Celts, 6–7
   tradition in art, 10, 11, 41
'Cenci, The', 128
Childe Harold's Pilgrimage, 134, 135, 136
connoisseurship, 52–3, 68–9, 88
Cortegiano, Il, 27, 34
country houses, 70–2, 85, 110
Crusades, 14, 16

Decameron, The, 23
Decline and Fall of the Roman Empire, The,
   57–9

Dido and Aeneas, 54
Dilettanti Society, 53, 79
Divine Comedy, The, 128–9, 130–1, 161–2
Don Juan, 135, 137
Dubliners, 154

Endimion and Phoebe, 42
'Endymion', 130, 131
'Epipsychidion', 129
Etruscan Places, 155
Extraordinary Women, 156

Faerie Queene, 31, 42
Family Reunion, The, 161
Finnegans Wake, 159

gardens, 109–19
   formal, 110–11
   landscape, 111–19
Gothic, 16–17, 40, 148
Gothic Revival, 74–5, 82–3
Grand Tour, 48–60, 68, 69, 71, 78, 90,
   96, 99, 112, 121, 123–4, 134–5,
   142
Greek language, 18, 22, 32–3, 36–7, 56,
   122, 129–30, 152, 161
guide books, 142

Hamlet, 33, 34
'Home Thoughts from Abroad', 144
humanism, 21–3, 43–4, 165
'Hyperion', 130–2

Imaginary Conversations, 146
interior decoration, 74, 77, 89
'Intimations of Immortality', 133

Julius Caesar, 32

'Kubla Khan', 133

Lady Chatterley's Lover, 155
landscape,
    appreciation of, 110, 112–15
    gardening, *see* gardens
    painting, 95–104, 107
    see also Picturesque
Latin, 2, 7, 9, 12, 13, 15, 17–18, 23, 32,
    36–7, 55–6, 149, 152, 161
'Lines Written among the Euganean
    Hills', 128
Lost Girl, The, 155
Lycidas, 37

Marino Faliero, 136
Merchant of Venice, The, 35
Modern Painters, 148
music, 11–12, 37–9, 54–5, 147, 157
myth, 33, 37, 130–3, 157–60

Neo-classicism, 75–84
Norman Conquest, 13–16

'Ode on a Grecian Urn', 131–2
'Ode to Autumn', 131
'Ode to Naples', 128
'Ode to the West Wind', 129
'Ode to Venice', 136
Old Calabria, 155
'On Seeing the Elgin Marbles', 132
opera, 54–5, 147
Oresteia, 161

Paradise Lost, 36, 37
Picturesque, 47, 81–2, 97, 100–1,
    112–19
'Pippa Passes', 145
Portrait of the Artist as a Young Man, A, 154
portraiture, 29, 39, 40, 76, 89, 90, 91,
    94–5, 103, 107
Pre-Raphaelite Movement, 105, 106, 148
Principe, Il, 26–7
Prometheus Unbound, 127, 130
puritanism, 35, 37, 40, 43–4, 46, 67, 89

railways, 142
Rape of Lucrece, The, 35
Reformation, 24, 43–4
Remarks on Several Parts of Italy, 47
Ring and the Book, The, 145
Risorgimento, 141, 144
Rococo, 75–6
Roman Britain, 6–8
Roman Catholic Church, 8–19, 46
Romanesque, 10–11, 16
Romanticism, 75, 114, 121–37, 139,
    146–7
Romola, 145
Rose and the Ring, The, 145
Ruins, 116–17

Samson Agonistes, 37
sculpture, 39–41, 90, 164–5
*Sentimental Journey through France and
    Italy*, 57
Song of Italy, 145
songs, 38–9
'Sonnets from the Portuguese', 144
'Sordello', 145
South Wind, 155
Stones of Venice, The, 149
'Sweeney Among the Nightingales', 160–
    161
Taming of the Shrew, The, 35
tourism, 142–3, 153
Tower, The, 163

Travels in France and Italy, 56
Tristram Shandy, 57
'Triumph of Life, The', 129
Troilus and Criseyde, 23

Ulysses (Joyce), 154, 159–60

'Ulysses' (Tennyson), 146

Venus and Adonis, 42
Vestal Fire, 156

Waste Land, The, 160, 161

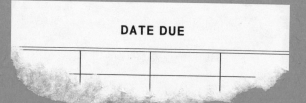

DATE DUE